Ruth, Clyde and Baby Jo

The Monkey's Nest

Jo Harris Shaw

Copyright © 2009 by Jo Harris Shaw

All rights reserved. No part of this book shall be reproduced or transmitted in any form or by any means, electronic, mechanical, magnetic, photographic including photocopying, recording or by any information storage and retrieval system, without prior written permission of the publisher. No patent liability is assumed with respect to the use of the information contained herein. Although every precaution has been taken in the preparation of this book, the publisher and author assume no responsibility for errors or omissions. Neither is any liability assumed for damages resulting from the use of the information contained herein.

ISBN 0-7414-5497-1

Author photo by Wayne Cathel.

Published by:
INFINITY
PUBLISHING
INFINITY PUBLISHING
1094 New DeHaven Street, Suite 100
West Conshohocken, PA 19428-2713
Info@buybooksontheweb.com
www.buybooksontheweb.com
Toll-free **(877) BUY BOOK**
Local Phone (610) 941-9999
Fax (610) 941-9959

Printed in the United States of America
Published January 2011

Acknowledgments

Photo: Wayne Cathel. *Belleair Images.com*

Editor: James E Shaw

Author: Jo Harris Shaw

Very special thanks to Susan Haley,
The Poet's Nook

Contents

The Monkey's Nest	1
Maw	7
Grandma Tippy Toe	13
The Devil Himself	17
Indians	22
Cal and Lucy	26
The Green Bike	38
The Equinox	42
When the Ghost Walks	48
Those Damn Harris Boys	52
Dolder's	65
Sisters	72
Cousins	84
The Figure Eight Kiss	92
Mom Dago	96
Train Yards	105
Old Man Glass	111
A Thorn in my Side	118
The Bradley Bunch	122
The Door Stop	128
Are You The Lady of The House?	132
Acid Holes	136
The Privy	140
Prisoner's Quarry	144
Wheels	150
The Ghosty Old House	153
Going Back	162
The McKinley Avenue Primer	168

The Monkey's Nest

When I was eight years old I was living in a haunted house with four brothers, a sister and a grandmother who read tea leaves and ranted about the Civil War. Aunts and uncles, cousins and friends and once a boarder, who left in the middle of the night, had all rented a room at the house at one time or another, but they never stayed for long.

My Southern mother and Cherokee father were good parents, but not by today's standards I suppose. Actually today they would have been in jail, and I would have missed all the fun, because they took me to bars on the weekends when I was a child, where nine times out of ten there was a brawl, with my father and his brother Cal smack in the middle of it.

Cal and his girlfriend Lucy dated off and on and he stayed at her goat farm when it suited him, or when he was hiding out from his ex wife Mary Lou.

Lucy was tall and big boned with freckles across her nose and cropped curly red hair. When she smiled, her eyes scrunched shut and she looked like a ten year old child.

I liked her the instant we met, she shook my hand like I was somebody important and she included me in the conversation she was having with mother. She was sweet as honey, but she had another side to her that really surprised me.

Like the time mother invited Lucy to our house for dinner one Sunday. It was nice, she told us funny stories about the goat farm, and of course Maw, my grandmother, had to throw her two cents worth in. She told us about the beautiful black horse she had bought for a song when she was a young woman, only to find out that it farted like a mule every time she hitched it to her buggy. "It was just *terrible* for courtin," she said.

We were all cackling and chattering like hens, until Cal decided he wanted to go to the San Margarita Bar and Grill, to meet his friend Dominick.

"Now Cal, don't you forget you're still on parole for that last brawl you was in," Lucy said in her soft voice, "and they'd send you back to the can plenty quick, if they caught you in a bar."

Cal's right eye squeezed shut and his lip curled as he pointed his finger at Lucy across the table, "Since when do I need you, to be tellin' ME, what the hell I can do, *woman*."

"Well somebody has to tell you!" Lucy leaned over the table until they were nearly eye to eye across the fried chicken and her big breasts hovered over the mashed potatoes. "Do you *want* to go back to jail?" she shouted.

Cal slammed his cup down on the lace table cloth sending brown coffee to the ceiling and jumped to his feet. Lucy ran around the table, countering him while he chased her.

"Cal. Come on man, sit down." Dad tried to reason, "Lucy didn't mean anything by that." I ran upstairs to my bedroom and closed the door; I knew how crazy Cal could be when he was mad. A few seconds later I heard thundering steps and then loud pounding on my door. It was Lucy.

"Jo Jo, let me in before he comes after me." Her voice sounded frantic, so I let her in and slammed the door while Cal shouted up the steps for her to come down, or he was coming up. I really liked Lucy and I was afraid he might harm her. She pressed herself against the door, and so did I, in case he tried to break it in.

"Lucy," I sobbed, "Are you awfully scared of Cal?"

"Oh honey," she hugged me, "I ain't scared of Cal at tall."

"You aren't?" She could have fooled me.

"Then why are you hiding in my room?"

"Because," she sighed, "if he takes a notion to hit me, I'll have to hit him back, and I don't want to hurt the little feller." I knew for a fact that the "little feller" could take care of himself in any situation that called for out and out brawling.

Take the day we spent at Lucy's goat farm for instance, we had been there all day when Cal and dad decided to go into town for beer and snacks. Mother said she wanted to ride along, and of course I had to go as well, because I didn't want to miss anything. Lucy decided to stay home and work on the new barn. She was doing most of the construction anyway.

She was sitting on the roof when we got ready to leave for town that afternoon. Her mouth was ringed with nails as she swung the big hammer to tack down the shingles.

As dad, Cal and mother piled into the car for the run into town, Lucy came down the ladder and called me over to her.

"Lord, Jo Jo" she whispered, "I sure am glad you're going to town with them. Maybe Cal won't stop anywhere and drink, with you along."

They did get the beer and snacks, but of course all good intentions were soon lost when Cal said he wanted to stop "for a quick one," in a bar called the Monkey's Nest on the west side of Columbus Ohio. Now it was midnight, and I was sleeping in a corner booth, my head resting on the table in the crook of my arm, when I heard a commanding voice speak to me.

"Go out and sit in the Plymouth, baby," the voice told me. My neck was stiff but I couldn't remember going to sleep, or where I was. I only knew that I was not at home in my own bed, and I wanted to be.

People were shouting at each other like barking dogs, but all I wanted to do was go back to sleep. It was 12:30 at night and I had to be up for Sunday school at 7:30 when Uncle John came to pick me up in his battered Ford with six other kids in the neighborhood. I had to go; I'd had perfect attendance since I was three. Uncle John was my father's uncle, and he was deacon of the Church of Christ in Christian Union in Valley View, where all the rich kids lived.

"Go on baby, sit in the car." It was my father Clyde speaking, after a night of drinking beer with Cal and my mother, Ruth. I could tell he was angry, but not with me. I followed his gaze of blue fire to a man across the room who was pointing the end of a beer bottle in our direction.

"You don't know jack shit Clyde," he yelled. "I can whip your ass in two minutes." There was a roar of encouraging shouts from his side of the room, and a backlash of threats from somewhere behind me. I had to wonder if this tattooed bully was stupid, or if he just didn't know that this slightly built fellow he was cussing so fervently was a feather weight boxing champion.

Hank Williams was singing about a cheating heart on the neon juke box and I wanted to stay and watch the action, because I knew what was coming, I had seen it before, a lot of times.

Cal drew trouble to him like a magnet draws metal. He liked to fight, his father had taught him, but his friends and family got pulled into his trouble as well, because Cal would give them the shirt off his back, and they loved him, if only for that reason.

"Baby," Dad leaned down and whispered in my ear, "You have to go out and sit in the car. Now go on, and be sure to lock the doors. I'll be out in a few minutes."

"But I don't want to," I whined,

"I want to stay here, with *mother*." I inched my head up to look at her, cast in amber through 6 empty beer bottles on the table before me. She was dreamy eyed, lost in her glass of beer, her beautiful *glow in the dark rose barrette*, glittering against her long chestnut hair.

"You go *now,* Jo! Sit in the car." Cal demanded, as a beer bottle sailed over his head and crashed against the wall. Seeing the brothers together reminded me of their Cherokee Bloodline, both were dark skinned and wildly handsome, except my father had eyes the color of cornflowers, a gift from his grandmother, who had inherited that dreaded drop of white blood from an Englishman. As Cal escorted me out to the Plymouth, all I could think about as I ran to the car and climbed into the back seat, was how I had let Lucy down.

A moment later glass exploded from the window of the bar and a chair shot across the hood of the car, taking the Venetian blinds with it. Looking through the newly opened window was like going to the Avondale Theater and watching a Bogart movie. I saw my father draw back his fist and punch the tattooed man in the face, twice. Blood shot from his mouth and he dipped out of view.

Another man flashed across the window with a screaming woman hanging on his back, hammering his head with a beer bottle.

Somewhere in the tangle of arms and legs, airborne chairs, and the shouts of fighting men, I caught a glimpse of a woman sitting at one of the back tables. I could barely see her through the raging battle and cigarette smoke as she calmly sat drinking a glass of beer. I screwed my eyes up real tight and pressed my face against the car window. Something was flashing in her hair. It was the *glow in the dark rose*! It was *mother!* Later, after it was all over with and everyone shook hands and patted each other on the back and my father finally got his nose to stop bleeding, we headed for home.

Somewhere in the distance I could hear the tiny whine of police sirens like alley cats on a fence, but as usual, they were too late. I was sleepy and full of orange soda and all I wanted to do was pee, and go to bed. We dropped Cal off at the farm and Lucy was standing on the front porch waiting for him. When she stepped down and put her hands on her hips, I knew she was really mad, and so did Cal.

"Now Cal, don't you go tellin' me you was out drinking again."

"Luc, I only had three beers, tops, but it won't happen again honey." He raised his right hand, "I swear to God." I had to smile, because I knew better. I knew it would start all over again the following Saturday, probably at the Wonder Bar this time though, or T.J.'s.

The Broken Knuckle and Little Nashville were off limits, because as mother pointed out to me one time, "Those bars are just too tough, to take a child into, honey."

Maw

Maw was my grandmother on mother's side of the family and even though I was the first surviving child my mother gave birth to, Maw was already 67 years old when I was born.

"Mommy was 42 when she had me," mother said, "I was a change of life baby, the last of ten.

She had to stay in a dark room for a month with all the shades pulled, and the doctor said if anyone even so much as rattled a paper bag in the room, that she might lose her mind.

I thought Maw was old when I was a baby and old when I was growing up in her house. I never saw her with the thick black hair that she wore to her waist when she was a young woman. I only saw her with the white hair, blunt cut to her ears, with silver rimmed glasses riding over toothless gums.

There were those occasions when Maw liked to reminisce about her youth.

"When I was a little girl," she'd tell me, "I had a white lace dress with a ruffled apron over it." I would close my eyes and try to see her as a little girl, but I just couldn't do it. I could see the white lace dress and little apron just fine, but they were on an old lady, a miniature Maw. To me, her hair had always been white. Except for the time when all of us kids had lice.

My younger brothers Jerry 6, and Leroy 5, had their heads shaved and didn't seem to mind, but I cried my heart out. It was the first time in two years that my hair was half way long, and I didn't look like Orphan Annie with one of my aunt Mattie's beauty shop permanents. But when mother blunt cut my hair to my ear lobes, I looked just like Maw.

"My hair was to my waist when I was your age," Maw told me.

"Then I took scarlet fever and the doctor told my mother that I would die if she didn't cut my hair. It was thick as a rope and it was holding the fever, you see. So they cut it all the way up to my ears, just like yours. Back then if you had short hair, they called you a Chippy."

"What's a Chippy?" I knew I shouldn't ask.

"It was a girl that liked men and the bottle. Now a days she'd be called a slut."

After hearing that story, I cried harder than ever.

"Dry your eyes and stop that crying." Cal scolded me.

"Those damn vermin'll be history by tonight." And he was right. Cal knew how they dealt with lice in the Big House. He dowsed all of our heads with kerosene. Maw got dowsed as well because Jerry and I and Leroy shared her big feather bed when we had house guests. And she was lousy as we were.

The kerosene not only killed the lice but it made our scalps shine like polished chrome, and it shrunk the skin so tight it pulled our eyes back to our temples. The kids at school laughed at us so hard that they had to hold their sides, and they started calling us the "Charley Chan Kids."

We had the last laugh though, when we were the only kids at Chicago Avenue Elementary that didn't have lice. Cal said the lice couldn't stand up on our shiny scalps, they just slid right off.

The kerosene treatment was done every Saturday afternoon for three weeks. Cal sat in a chair in the backyard with a tiny black comb and we took turns sitting on the ground between his knees.

After the dowsing he'd put on Maw's big magnified silver glasses that made his eyes look like enormous centipedes and he'd go over every inch of our heads. Then he'd comb and comb and comb.

Everything in the house was washed with kerosene and washed again in lye soap and rinsed in vinegar water.

The walls and floor was wiped down with kerosene and soap, and then rinsed and dried until finally the lice was gone, for good. Smokers had to go outside to take a drag though, because Dad said the house and everybody in it, could blow up like the Hindenburg.

The "treatment" turned my hair a pretty auburn with red and gold highlights, but Maw was a different story. Not only did she look Oriental with her shiny tight scalp pulling her eyes back to her temples, but her white hair was a bright tinny gold, and shiny like the hair on my doll. It was wild too, arching out from her head like elephant grass. She brushed and brushed until it lay flat, but by the time she came downstairs it had sprung out again and she looked like a wild jungle lion. She discovered she couldn't wear her navy blue hat either, the one with the veil and little velvet flowers sewn delicately on the sides.

Even hat pins wouldn't hold it down. Her hair had a life of its own, and by the time she walked to the bus line, her wild hair had slowly inched the hat to the top of her hair ends. She said she caused a three car pile up just waiting at the bus stop one day.

But strangest of all though, was her face. It was completely free of any lines or wrinkles, like skin drawn over a drum. It was a startlingly young face, but without teeth, because Maw wouldn't wear dentures.

It was scary too, especially at night when she came down the long shadowy hall upstairs to the back bedroom, and Jerry and I and Leroy were already in her bed. Her shadow cast before her on the wall, like a gigantic toothless monster, with wiry hair and flashing eyes, reflected from her silver rimmed glasses. Even Jerry, at five years old, who wasn't afraid of anything this side of hell, would grab my arm in the dark bed and say, "SSShit!".

Nearly every Sunday, Maw would go for her weekly drive with Zeta and Nora, her two daughters, in Zeta's big green Buick. Zeta and her husband Floyd owned a restaurant on the hilltop and they lived in the prestigious Valley View section of town, in a dream house with a fairy garden and roses big as tea cups. Mother always said that Zeta and Nora were refined, they knew all about social graces and which fork to use and when.

Nora had moved in with Zeta after her husband died in California, and I thought they must be very wealthy because they took trips to Arizona and Michigan every year and they wore silver belts and Indian jewelry.

They always took Maw for a drive in the country, or to Jean and Lou's Barbecue & Grill in the little town of Dublin Ohio. They were both as devoted to her as if she was the Queen Mother, and Maw expected nothing less from all of her children.

Afterwards it was a long drive in the country to see the monument of Chief Leather Lips, or down to the zoo by Hoover Dam. When Aunt Zeta would bring her 10 year old daughter Joan along, I was allowed to go as well.

One Sunday morning Maw called downstairs and asked mother to come up to her room, and of course I trailed along as well, to see what was going on,

"How do I look?" Maw patted her hair in the bedroom mirror.

"Mommy you look just fine."

"My hair isn't too yella, is it?"

"No mommy, your hair isn't yellow at all." Mother glanced at me and bit her lip.

It wasn't yellow. It was *orange*. With big fat brassy streaks. When Zeta drove up, Maw ran to get her purse, then she nabbed me by my dress sleeve.

"Not a word about the lice! You hear me? Maybe they won't take notice of anything." Her shiny scalp was reflecting the overhead light in the hall, but I wasn't going to tell her.

When we came downstairs Nora took one look at Maw and grabbed hold of the chair back with both hands.

"Mommy!" Her eyes bugged, "What did you do to yourself?" Nora had lived in California and she was prone to fainting if anything upset her. I thought she might faint now.

"What in the world have you done to your hair?" Zeta rushed over for a closer look, her eyes as wide as Nora's. Cousin Joan leaned towards me and sniffed, her brows furrowed. She had a way of getting things out of me; I would have to be *very* careful.

Maw was busy jamming her hands into her sweater sleeves and hurrying to the door. The sweater was riding up and over the hump on her back, but she didn't stop to make any adjustments.

"If you want me to go and eat with you, then we have to leave now, or I'm stain' here. I don't want to miss my radio program tonight, so let's get a move on."

Everyone rushed out the door like old time movies, climbed in the car and Zeta peeled out, gravel and smoke flying off the back tires. We were both severely interrogated in the Buick, but my lips were sealed and I was proud of Maw's loyalty to the Harris family as she sat up front between Zeta and Nora, looking like an escaped lion with her mane of wild hair. Nora wanted to know everything that was going on, all the details, and why.

"Mommy," Nora patted Maw's arm affectionately, "tell me what happened to your pretty white hair. I feel like something is going on and you know I have a gift for intuition."

Maw viewed Nora from the bottom of her glasses. It was like the queen getting ready to announce a beheading.

"You've got a gift alright Nora, but it isn't for intuition, it's more like *suspicion*. Why do you always have to know the piss and guts of everything?" "Besides," Maw folded her arms, "it's none of your damn business what I did with my hair. But the truth is," everyone leaned forward, "I went to see Mattie at her shop, and she did a new Hollywood beauty treatment on me."

"You DO like it, don't you?" Maw frowned. You could have heard crickets in the silence, but Zeta with her customary grace, finally spoke.

"Mommy I think if you like it, that's all that matters. I just want to know what Mattie used on your face though, you look ten years younger."

We never went to Jean and Lou's Barbecue & Grill. Both Zeta and Nora had a sudden craving for Chop Suey and took us to Ding Lee's on Broad Street. It was my first taste of the Orient. Well, almost.

Grandma Tippy Toe

Dad took the bus downtown nearly every Saturday to his sister Mattie's big apartment building, to see his mother Mary. She was tiny and thin with a long trail of white hair that hung down her back like cigarette smoke. When she walked it was quietly, with her heels slightly elevated, as if she was in a library and didn't want to disturb anyone. Maybe that was why I had always called her Grandma Tippy Toe.

Her mother was Cherokee and Dad said it was Tippy Toe's blood remembering when her people had to walk through the forest without snapping a twig or rustling a leaf, least they scare away the wild turkey and deer. But she wasn't in the forest anymore, now she lived in her daughter Mattie's attic.

I loved Tippy Toes apartment, it was small, tightly packed and tidy, like going into a rabbit hole. Dad and I would walk up the two flights of stairs in Mattie's building; turn left and go up four narrow steps to a landing and then up four more steps to a small door leading to the attic.

It was one big room with a kitchen sink, a small table with four chairs, a little white refrigerator and a doll sized stove, with her brass bed tucked under the rafters in the far corner.

There was a big oak dresser with a round mirror sitting cross cornered at the other end of the room where she had stacked my father's old school books behind it. I spent Saturday afternoons in that dim corner hunched on a footstool reading, while they visited. She made lunch, with red bean salad, fried sausages, and pound cake with very weak coffee.

Next to the oak dresser there was a big octagon window edged with stained glass that looked out over the city.

"See the funeral home across the street?" Tippy Toe pointed out the window. "That is where Mattie worked to pay her way through beauty school. She dressed the hair of the dead for their journey to the Spirit world."

One floor down from the attic in the hall there was a bathroom, and I was allowed to use it once and *only* once when we visited. And *then only*, if I was in agony and had to hold the pee in by crossing my legs.

Dad said it was "green" (his word for rude,) to use the bathroom when visiting the homes of others. We didn't have an indoor toilet, so I was fascinated with Mattie's lavender scented bathroom and maroon tiled floor.

If I peed quickly, I had time to go downstairs and look around in Mattie's huge living room before Dad came looking for me. She lived on the first floor and rented out the rest of the building. It was magnificent with its 16 ft. ceilings and richly polished floors, the windows draped with red velvet curtains, and everything smelled like cinnamon candy.

But Mattie was a tosser, and everything she brought home was still lying where she had dropped it three weeks before, usually on her dining room table or the sofa.

She couldn't find anything under the six bolts of material she bought to have Oriental silk curtains, custom made, boxes of merchandise, new shoes, clothes, newspapers, magazines, bills, her mink stole that she thought was lost. So finally she hired a housekeeper, a short stocky woman with dyed black hair and a turned up nose, named Mary Jane.

Mary Jane was with Mattie a week when she developed a mad crush on Herb, my father's younger, very good looking, and alcoholic brother.

Mattie spent hundreds of dollars trying to convert her brother Herb into a socially acceptable person that would not embarrass her by spending every weekend in the lockup.

After all, she was a regular in the society page with her mink stole draped around her jeweled neck. Herb had the use of the small guest bedroom in Mattie's apartment, just off the dining room. It was her way of trying to keep him in line that is until Mary Jane saw him.

Mary Jane and I had something in common though. She hated me, and I hated her.

"Don't come down here snooping around again, if you know what's good for you, kid." She told me this, once, when she caught me running my fingers over a bolt of red silk that Mattie had tossed on her sofa a month before. I didn't want to take anything, I knew better, but it was so beautiful I couldn't resist touching it.

She fastened chubby fingers around my arm and pushed me out the door into the hall. When I told Tippy Toe about it, she scolded me, sounding like a Cherokee grandmother.

"Child, you are too curious, and you must learn to keep your own council and not tell everything you know. I will tell you an ancient wisdom, now listen closely. A wise old owl sat in an oak, the more he heard the less he spoke, the less he spoke the more he heard, you should be wise like that old bird."

The next time I went downstairs to Mattie's. I opened the door a crack and peered into the living room. It was in shadows, the Venetian blinds pulled shut behind the heavy drapes.

I saw nothing to interest my curiosity but as I was closing the door, I heard the soft tinkle of giggling in Herb's bedroom. I knew I should go, and I started to. But I couldn't.

I tiptoed across the dimly lit living room and into the dining room to the half closed door of Herb's bedroom and looked in. Mary Jane was on the bed, in her girdle, straddling Herb.

Every time he bounced her up and down, the fat under her bra quivered, and she chortled, like a morning dove. It was really more than I wanted to see, but when I turned on my heel to leave, I bumped into the dining room table. The tall crystal candle holder in the center of the table tipped and swayed, clashing the dangling prisms together like church bells. The chortling stopped abruptly and I heard the mattress squeak.

I grabbed the candle holder with a death grip and set it upright again, but not before I heard Mary Jane's feet hit the floor. Streaking across the living room, I rode the fat throw rug like a surf board on the polished floors and eased out the door, closing it softly behind me. I was up the two flights of stairs and behind Tippy Toe's dresser with my nose in a book, when Mary Jane knocked on the door. Dad answered it.

"Ohhh, Mr. Harris," she puffed, out of breath, her chignon hanging on the side of her ear, "I was umm…just looking for Mattie," she smiled in her candy coated voice as she craned her short neck, "sorry I bothered you."

Her little pig eyes darted until they found mine. I smiled and waved. I was the owl, and it was *my* secret.

When dad and I finally left Tippy Toe, Mattie stepped into the hall from the beauty shop to talk to him

"Oh Clyde! Did I mention how *well* Herb is behaving himself lately?"

"No, but I'm sure glad to hear that, Mattie," he said. I could have told her how well he was behaving, if she had just asked *meee*.

The Devil Himself

One day I found a faded picture of my dad's father, Calvin. He was sitting on the front porch of a white frame farm house surrounded by his wife and children. He was dark skinned with black hair and a full mustache. Not a *single* person in the picture was smiling, and I wanted to know why.

"Why does everybody in this picture look so mean?" I asked mother.

"Probably because your grandfather Calvin was in it. That man was the devil himself! And that was a long time before he was blind too."

"But how did he get to be blind?" I asked.

Mother was quiet while she cleared the supper dishes from the kitchen table and wiped the oil cloth clean. She was pondering. "He worked on the Ohio River for a while. He was a cook on one of those barges. Your father went with him a couple of times when he was a kid, but he said he didn't have the stomach for it.

Clyde told me that the men along the river were the toughest people he ever met, just plain crazy. He said that they were all the time fishing bodies out of the water, people that got themselves stabbed or shot or just beaten to death."

"Anyway, the old man loved to fight so he fit right in with that group. But one time he picked on this kid, a young farm boy from back in one of those southern Ohio hollows. There was a big fight and Calvin broke the kid's nose. Well that should have ended it, but the kid grabbed Calvin by the neck, and stuck his thumb, in his eye."

"In his *eye?*" I was horrified, this happened to Victor Manure (my name for him,) in "Samson and Delilah," when he had his eyeballs ripped out, except he wasn't in West Virginia.

"That's right, he just pulled that eye right out of the socket." Mother stuck her finger in her mouth and pulled it out, making a loud popping sound while I flattened myself against the wall.

"Did Calvin run home and try to put his eyeball back in the socket?"

"The old man? You've got be kidding, he wouldn't leave a fight if they sawed his leg off. No, he just reared up and bit that kid's ear, right off."

My lips rolled together like a chimp's. I knew from Sunday school about an eye for an eye, but an *ear* for an eye?

"Aww..he was nearly blind in one eye to begin with, and now he couldn't see out of the other one because it wasn't there, it was just a black sunken hole. Mrs. Harris, your grandmother, had to take a job doing laundry across the Ohio River because he couldn't work. She had a small boat that she rowed to and from work. That was the Indian in her I guess. Anyway, more often than not, he took her money when she got paid and she couldn't do anything about it."

"But why was he so mean?"

"Because, I *told* you, he was the devil himself." Mother threw all the silverware into the sink with a big splash and started washing them vigorously.

"He never liked me," she said. "But I wasn't afraid of him like the rest of the family. When he shouted, everybody came running to see what he wanted, or he threw a fit. I'd seen him break everything in the house when he was in a rage."

I was pretty far along with Lester, my first baby, and Clyde was working on the WPA. I hardly ever saw him, we were just two kids trying to stay alive back then like everybody else during the depression." She started scooping coffee grounds into the big ranch pot, and after filling it with water she set it on the stove to boil.

"Anyway, Clyde came home one day in a fury. He said his father was dying, and the old man told him that he'd been hearing rumors about me. He said he heard I was seen with other men while Clyde was working, and his father doubted the baby was his. We had a big fight and he took off, he said he'd sooner be digging ditches than to be living with a woman he couldn't trust."

"After he left I cried until I was nearly sick, but pretty soon I started to feel my blood boiling. It just went "WHOOM," she smacked her hands together and I jumped. "It was like a wild fire pounding in my ears," she said. "I decided I had to go see that old man for myself."

"They lived about three miles down the road and I took off walking as fast as I could go, I would have been running if I hadn't been pregnant."

"I heard they had him propped up in a chair in the living room. I figured he was too hateful to die in bed like anybody else. Clyde's mother was sitting on the front porch and when she saw me coming she jumped up and ran over to me."

"Ruth, honey," she said to me, "don't go in there. Let it go. I know none of that trash is true because I know you. Besides, he doesn't want to be bothered, and he'll be terrible hard on you. You have to think of that baby now."

"Now I don't have anything against you, Mrs. Harris," I told her, "because I know the shame you had to take from him all these years, but I *am* going to see him, and that's that."

"She nodded her head and I went on into the house, I think she was glad that somebody was finally going to stand up to him. When I walked in he looked surprised."

"Did you come over here to watch me die, girl?"

"If that was the case old man, I'd be grinning from ear to ear." I told him. He shook his head and kind of laughed, "You always was a feisty one," he said.

I went to where he was propped against the pillows in a big chair, and I leaned down *real* close to his face. He smelled just like death. "I came here to tell you something." said.

I interrupted her, "But what does death smell like?" I asked her. I needed to know, in case I was ever around it, but she gave me "the look" so I shut up.

"Like I was telling you, I got real close to him and I said, "Well old man, your son believed you, because you swore on your death bed. But you know you lied, and I know it too."

"What did the devil himself, say?" I was unconsciously drying the silverware, a chore I hated and usually weaseled out of when I could.

"He was looking at me with that one glazed eye, and he started laughing." she said.

"It was *plain old gossip,* girl, besides....I figured my son had a right to know. I told him you was just a young ignorant girl, and he'd better beat some damn sense into you before you ruined his good name,...but hell, I can see I've hurt your tender feelings. He started wheezing real bad then and said to me, "Can you find in your heart to forgive a dying old man?"

"I thought about the terrible lies he told about me even before I was married, and the way he treated Mrs. Harris, and all the fights Clyde and I had over him in the past."

"What did you say,?" I asked her.

"Well. I said, "HELL NO!" And I walked out."

I couldn't close my mouth! "But... he was *dying!*" I choked. "You couldn't even forgive him when he was *dying?*" I was only eight years old. I was at her mercy for another ten years, at least. What if *I* ever made her that mad at me? The thought caused my Adams apple to quiver.

"He was going to die anyway, whether I forgave him or not."

"And you really, really, really couldn't forgive him?" I squealed.

"No! I really, really, really couldn't forgive him." She examined the spoons I was drying. "Don't forget to dry those handles too," I dried them, I was afraid not to.

Indians

Where my father's parents were Cherokee and Sioux, mixed with white, mother's mix was a strong Virginia and English with a little German and Spanish for flavor. She said her kids were dark skinned Indians who liked sauerkraut and fried chicken with Spanish rice.

Dad's oldest brother Homer showed the strong Cherokee bloodline in his chiseled features and dark skin. Only his short white hair and gray eyes revealed the intrusion of the white man in his blood. He spoke slowly and distinctly, but with great force, like Red Cloud, and he used his hands when he spoke, as all the brothers did.

If we were visiting him, and he sent me to the store for a loaf of bread or milk, I felt like I was on a mission for the tribe.

"I come for MILK, BREAD!" I demanded from the old man at the store.

"Homer's niece, right?" He'd say. Herb was the youngest of the Harris boys and he was Hollywood handsome with his black wavy hair and dark skin. You would never guess he was an alcoholic; he dressed like a fashion model, wearing expensive cream colored suits, silk shirts and

Italian shoes. Except when he was on a toot, and then he lost particles of his clothing all over town.

Once he came to our house wearing red velvet shoes curled up at the ends with tassels on them. He was walking on his toes like a werewolf, with his arms held out so he could maintain his balance.

"Where in the hell did you get those shoes?" Mother asked him.

"I don't know, Ruth." Herb laughed in his deep chuckle, "I woke up this morning outside of a movie theater on the East side, and I was wearing these damn shoes.

"Seems like I remember a Shriners convention or something like that. Hell, I'll have to wear them over to Matte's until my Italian shoes show up again."

Maw made him eggs and bacon with her strong "hair on your chest" coffee, and after breakfast he went upstairs to take a nap in the back bedroom. About half an hour later Jerry came running into the kitchen, his pointed eyebrows perked into his hairline.

"Herb's dead," he announced.

Mother, Maw, me and Jerry ran up the steps and crowded into the back bedroom. Herb was laying on his back with his mouth slacked open, and his glassy eyes staring at the ceiling.

"Oh my God." Mother walked over and looked down at him, tears filling her eyes. "How will I ever tell Clyde." I was crying too and so was Jerry. She bent to pull the sheet over his eyes and reared back with her hand over her mouth.

"Hells fire! He's not dead. He's sleeping. And his breath smells like after shave." Herb had guzzled both bottles of *Old Spice* from the hall pantry.

"Dammit to *hell!*" Dad yelled, when he found out.

Cal (the louse man,) spent a good deal of time with us, so I knew him better than the others. Where Herb was polished silk, Cal was rough around the edges. With his dark skin and short cropped black hair, he was Charles Bronson.

When he stayed with us between his prison "vacations" everything in our house sparkled, he was an absolute nut about neatness. Marrying Lucy and moving to the hills settled him down but he still went into town and raised hell.

Where the brothers were handsome, the three sisters got left out in the rain. Mattie showed the broad face and nearly flat nose of the Mongolian stock which is a part of the Indian bloodline dating back 15,000 years. Myrtle, the middle sister was tall and paper thin with black hair around her shoulders, dark skin and a sharp nose. We didn't see the sisters unless there was a crisis, a funeral, or a near death experience, then one of them *migh*t come over.

When Myrtle came to our house mother would say, "Well, here comes Olive Oil."

Elizabeth, the youngest of the three girls was a spinster and the better looking of the three. She was quiet and polite, and wore her dark hair twisted at the back of her neck. She had a moderate overbite like a little chipmunk and she peered at the world out of bottle thick glasses. Elizabeth looked harmless enough but underneath she was tough as nails.

She owned a small deli on the west side of Columbus where she sold meat, canned goods and fresh bakery items.

One night she was robbed at gun point by a young boy. He took all the money she had in the register and apologized to her three times before he ran out the door.

Elizabeth weighed 109 pounds but she chased him for three blocks until he finally had to stop for a breath and we waited for the police arrive. Later in the month when the boy went before the judge, she was called in to testify.

"The boy and I had a nice long talk while we were waiting for the police to come," she told the judge, "and I think he deserves another chance. I'm willing to see that he gets it."

"What do you propose to do?" The judge leaned over his bench to look down at Elizabeth.

"I propose, to give him a job in my deli."

"Miss Harris, do you really want to do that, after this young man tried to rob you?"

"Your Honor, I consider myself a good judge of character and I believe he won't let me down, I think he was desperate and acted without thinking."

The judge shook his head, "Well now I've seen it all," he said.

The boy worked in the deli faithfully until Elizabeth sold it to him two years later.

Cal and Lucy

Cal was staying with us for a while. He'd just come out of the Ohio State Penitentiary after serving 30 days for non-support, again. His ex-wife Mary Lou would have him picked up if he was a few months late with the support check, and he usually was, so it was back in the can for poor Cal.

He got so he knew most of the officers down town by their first names though and they seemed to like him, even when they had to handcuff and haul him off to jail. Like the time he was helping Maw with the laundry and we were singing *You are my Sunshine*.

Cal was wearing one of Maw's aprons with the ruffles over the shoulders. He was hanging up the laundry and I was handing him the clothes pins when two men in brown uniforms came around the side of the house. They had sheriff's badges pinned on their shirt pockets.

I puckered up because I knew what they wanted, but Cal just shook his head and ran his fingers through his short hair.

One of the men was paper thin with his dark hair combed forward in a bush on his forehead. The other guy was round as a *Ritz* cracker with a belly that swelled out and hung over his belt. Thin black hair was plastered against his head and a tiny black mustache seemed to grow out of his nose like a mouse peeking out of a hole. They resembled someone I knew, but I couldn't think who it was. Then I remembered, it was Laurel and Hardy.

"Cal Harris," Laurel laughed, "if you ain't the damndest looking fella I ever seen, dressed up like a woman and hangin' out laundry."

"We hate like hell to take you away from your *womanly* duties Cal, but that ex of yours has a warrant issued for you again." They grinned at Cal while I dug the heels of my hands into my eye sockets and cried.

Cal patted me on the head and untied his apron. He tossed it in the clothes basket and walked over to the two officers with his hands held forward, and they slapped the cuffs on him.

"Don't feel bad, Gus, let's just get it over with." Cal turned to go just as Maw flew out of the back door waving her cane like a saber.

"You sonsabitches! Can't you leave that boy in peace?"

"You just better go back in the house right now, grandma." Hardy said.

Her eyes narrowed as she shot off the porch, and in a flash, she grabbed Hardy's tiny mustache and twisted. He squealed like a pig but she wouldn't let go, pointing her cane at Cal.

"You boys can have him, (she let go of Hardy) when that load of clothes is hung, and not before." There was absolute silence as the officers glanced at each other and their eyes narrowed. For a long moment I wondered if they were going to shoot Maw.

Laurel finally stepped forward, unlocked Cal's cuffs, and they both resolutely sat down on the back steps, until he had finished hanging out the wash. Then they handcuffed him again and took him back to the Big House for his 30 day visit.

Maw baked cookies and mother and I took them to the Penitentiary along with a carton of Lucky Strikes. Maw said she might as well bake a whole load of cookies and just keep them on hand for Cal's "visits."

But that was before Lucy set Cal straight and saved him from himself. That was before he was ready to give up the wild side of life for the love of a good woman, or that's what Aunt Ethyl said, anyway.

In the meantime he just floated from Lucy's farm to our house and back to the Big House again.

Maw loved having Cal stay with us, he was a top notch housekeeper, an excellent cook, and he knew all the gossip in town. Maw said it was like having an ugly woman in the house to share the chores and cooking with, and she loved the afternoon lunches. Cal made hot buttermilk biscuits with white sausage gravy, pan bread with strawberry jam and "hair on your chest" strong coffee topped off with "who done what, to who's wife, and where they done it."

Lucy got tired of Cal's wild drinking and hanging out with his friends in San Margarita. When he stayed at her farm he was coming home drunk at all hours, acting mean like his father. He failed miserably though, when Lucy nearly broke his nose one night after he took a swing at her.

"Oh Ruffy, I never wanted to hurt Cal." Lucy sobbed on mother's shoulder the next day. "But he just kept comin' after me, and I had to stop him. He knows better than to treat me like his daddy treated his mother. Oh Lord," she wailed, "I mighta killed him."

Cal wouldn't leave the farm so Lucy moved in with us. I was glad, Cal needed to be knocked down a peg or two, but Lucy was sleeping in my room and I was having to sleep with Maw and Jerry. If you didn't go to bed when Maw went up the steps at 9:27, you could forget it.

The United States Marines could not get into Maw's bedroom, or at least I thought so. Not after she performed the "Ritual." The Ritual included three weapons that she kept in her night stand. After she greased us with Vicks Salve until our eyes watered and tucked the heavy quilt tight against our ears, she pulled the three knives out of the night stand drawer.

One knife was placed across the top of the door knob and slid into the door framing. The other two were placed above it at precisely the same distance apart. The door was tested for endurance and this was a ritual in itself.

She pulled three times on the door knob, ducking down each time to look under the bed like some mad whirling dervish. Finally the light was out, and we could go to sleep.

Unless there was a crisis and she had to open the door, then all hell broke loose.

And the second night Lucy stayed with us, there was a crisis. Our doors were never locked, so Cal came in the house at 2:00 in the morning. He was drunk and yelling for Lucy as he came stomping up the steps.

He must have thought Lucy was in Maw's room because she wouldn't answer him when he called her name and banged on my bedroom door at the top of the steps. Certain that she was in the back bedroom he stormed down the hall and pounded on Maw's door.

"Luuuuucy! You better let me in! I know damn well you're in there!" Maw did not wake up easily, and if she was suddenly jarred awake she could be dangerous, especially if she was having a bad dream.

One afternoon our cousin Red, tapped her on the arm while she was snoring on the back porch in the oak rocking chair. She reared up, grabbed him by the neck and nearly choked him to death before we could wake her.

"I don't know, I must have been dreaming about Atlanta burning.... and I thought you was a damn Yankee," she said.

Now, as Cal yelled and pounded on her door, she sat up in bed stiff as a store mannequin. In the bright moonlight coming through the window I could see that she was only half awake as she rolled out of bed and rooted around on the floor for her house slippers. At that moment Cal slammed himself against the bedroom door and split the frame.

All three of the knives she had stuck in the door shot across her head, dipped under our noses in formation like the Blue Angels, and crashed against the wall with a clatter.

Maw raised her head up, she was wide awake now, and there was murder in her eyes. The Confederate brow rose until it disappeared into her hairline, and a long string of toothless cuss words came out of her mouth. She yanked the door open and Cal fell, landing at her feet.

Before he could get up she found one of her heavy, lace up the front shoes, the ones with the wide one inch heels, and tattooed Cal's head like a woodpecker. Twice she hit him on his already bruised nose, which made Jerry and I both suck our teeth and groan in sympathy.

All the while he crawled drunkenly around the bedroom floor, "ouching" and "ohhhing" every time she struck a blow. He couldn't crawl fast enough to get away from her, but finally he found the door and tripped down the hall to the stairs.

Maw hung over the banister still holding the shoe. "Goddamn savage heathen!" She hollered after him, "They oughta put you on a reservation where you belong!"

Dad said if the Indians had captured Maw they would have brought her right back!

Early the next morning while the birds were still chirping there was a knock on the back door. It was Cal. He was sober and looked to be sincerely regretful, with visible knots on his forehead and his nose swollen until it blacked both of his eyes, but I had seen that before too. The truth was, I had seen him look worse!

He hung his head down until it nearly touched his chest bone. But there was something new; he had brought flowers for Maw and Lucy. I squinted my eyes, they looked suspiciously like old Hump Smith's American Beauties and purple Iris's to me. She lived in the alley behind us.

"Well if you ain't the sorriest looking pup I ever seen." Maw shook her head and opened the screen door.

"Get in here and sit down while I find a poultice to put on that nose before it drops off your face. Then you wouldn't have anything to stick into other people's business in the middle of the night, now would you?"

Cal's flowers, and a big hug, along with his heartfelt promises never to drink again, won Maw over, and no-one was more surprised than I was. Even Lucy was sucked in by his sterling charm. I gave him two weeks to stay on the good behavior band wagon, and that was a stretch.

Later that summer Cal and Lucy were quietly married at the court house.

Lucy sold her goat farm and she and Cal moved to Marietta Ohio, back in the hills, so far back that it was five miles to their mailbox. They had bought 150 acres with a lovely old two story house on top of a mountain. The front porch had a wicker swing and in the evening you could look down into a purple mist filled valley of farm houses and streams. In the morning the white mist rose out of the abyss like a thin lace wedding veil.

There was a huge blackberry patch in the woods, apple trees, and wild herbs of nearly every variety. They had four cows, a huge old bull with curls hanging over his forehead and a big ring in his nose. Chickens, goats, three horses and a feisty mule. And there were cats, everywhere. And dogs, everywhere. People abandoned them in the mountains and they made a bee line for Lucy. She even adopted an old white horse that was on its way to the glue factory. It was so hopelessly sway backed that when Jerry rode it you couldn't see the top of his head.

Cal invited us to come and spend the weekends because they had four big bedrooms and 150 acres to run around in. All of us loved visiting the farm, except dad. He loved the farm, but he wouldn't eat unless mother agreed to help Lucy cook. He thought Lucy wasn't clean in her kitchen habits. I had to agree with him, on one occasion in particular.

"Hey Lucy," mother said one Saturday morning when she was getting ready to fry a mess of eggs and bacon for breakfast. "Where is your big skillet, hon?"

"It's over the stove," Lucy called from the next room, "on that green shelf, Ruffy."

When mother pulled the skillet down it was heavy and there was a good reason. Curled inside of it fast asleep, was a yellow kitten.

"Am I suppose to fry this for breakfast?" Mother yelled from the kitchen.

Lucy took the skillet from mother's hand and poured the kitten out like pancake batter onto the kitchen table, careful not to wake him from his nap, then she took her apron and wiped around the inside of the skillet and handed it back to mother.

"There you go, Ruffy," she whispered. "Now you can fry them eggs."

Lucy was like a big kid, she was afraid of everything, but she was especially afraid of the dark. One weekend we stayed at the farm and it was well past dark when Cal asked her to go down the mountain to the little store in the flat land and get some beer and snacks. Cal and dad were both waist deep under the hood of the old tractor in the barn, trying to get it to start.

My brother Leroy was five years old and sick with a cold and a high fever and mother didn't want to leave him, so Lucy called me to her side when she came out on the porch with the keys to the Jeep.

"Go with me will you, Jo Jo?" I was ready for bed but there was something in her eyes that reminded me of my little brother Earl when he was scared. But Earl was scared of his shadow.

Earl was so scared, it made him scared just to think about being that way.

"Okay," I nodded, and climbed into the Jeep next to her. The sky was velvet black, no moon or stars and not a flicker of light lay beyond the scope of her headlights as we started out. Lucy looked over at me with her mouth pulled tight.

"I was reading in the Farmer's Almanac where it said that this is the dark of the moon."

Maw always said that strange things are generated when the moon is hiding, and evil abounds. I felt like the night was eating the Jeep as we drove into it, like some huge hungry beast with its mouth open. The slender arms of tree branches reached out from either side of the narrow dirt road that angled down the lane to the mailbox.

From there, we took another dirt road that would lead to the paved route into town. I felt goose bumps dance up my spine like bubbles in a glass of ginger ale. Lucy was right about one thing, the hills were spooky in the dark.

"Thanks for comin' with me." The whites of Lucy's eyes reflected the green glow from the dashboard. "I have to be honest with you, Jo Jo. I don't like driving these hills, even in the daylight. I've seen some things in these parts that just wasn't natural."

There was a little quiver at the edge of her voice and I was surprised to see her so scared. I gripped the sides of the seat when she floored the Jeep, spinning the back wheels on the dirt road that wound around the mountain. The headlights touched neon eyes of night critters as we flew over pot holes and spun gravel on the hairpin curves.

Halfway down the mountain fog rolled across the road in a thick blanket, rising up from the valley. Lucy shot over a rise in the road and I felt the tires leave the ground. For a second I thought I was going to be air borne too, but I held tight to the handle on the dash and when we landed I ended up on the floor.

"I'm sorry, are you okay, honey?" Lucy looked over at me as I scrambled back into my seat.

"Yeah, I think so." I was examining my right arm to see if it was still working. That was when I saw the old woman. She was bent over a cane, walking at the edge of the road, clutching a shawl under her chin that covered her hair and draped around her shoulders.

She turned around when our headlights touched her and threw up her hand in a friendly gesture. I was sure we were going to stop, but to my amazement Lucy stepped on the gas again, making the Jeep lurch forward and skid on the upcoming curve.

"Lucy! Aren't you going to stop?" My voice jerked as I was bounced around in the seat of the rocketing Jeep.

"I can't." She glanced over at me and turned away without another word.

"But she's out in the middle of nowhere." I looked back in the fog and she was gone, already swallowed up and left alone, out there in that awful darkness.

It wasn't like Lucy to be so cruel. Could this be the same woman who took in all the strays in Southern Ohio?

"But why couldn't you just stop and pick her up?" The lights of the tiny town came into view and we were both silent as she drove up to the general store.

It was the local gas station, post office and grocery store and it looked like something out of a Norman Rockwell calendar for August. Back of the counter putting cans on a wooden shelf was a red faced man in a blue checked shirt and bib overhauls. He nodded when we came in the door.

"Miss Lucy, you shore are a sight for sore eyes." One side of his face jutted out of proportion at a crazy angle and he transferred his "chaw" to the other side before he attempted a stained smile.

"Hey there, Kaiser, hope the family is doin' well. This is my little niece, Jo Jo. Cal's brother Clyde, you know? They come in for the weekend."

"Lucy, I heard tell you was taken' in two old war vets for boarders." The chaw went to the other side of his face again, punching that side out like a balloon.

"I was thinkin' on that idea pretty strong, we sure could use the extra income."

Lucy grabbed candy bars, Pepsi Cola's and twelve bottles of beer; potato chips, pretzels and two big dill pickles from the barrel. She ran and gathered up three loaves of bread and slapped them down on the counter by the big jar of pickled pigs feet.

"Kaiser, could you slice me up about three pounds of that ham and two pounds of your good bologna? And I'd be obliged if you could put a step on it too, I'm in an awful big hurry."

Lucy was always country slow, like she had all the time in the world, but now she was acting like the store was on fire, I had never seen her like that before.

She kept walking over and looking out of the window, biting her finger nails and pacing the floor.

Kaiser on the other hand, moved like molasses as he sliced the meat rhythmically, watching as each piece rolled off the long loaf and landed on the butchers paper before pushing it through the slicer again. When he finally came back to the counter and began cranking the handle up and down on the ancient adding machine, he found a need to comment on each item while Lucy impatiently tapped her toe on the worn linoleum.

"That'd be six dollars and 42 cents, give or take a nickel." When he spit in the brass pot back of the counter I heard it "ping." He winked at me as he wiped his mouth on his sleeve.

Lucy quickly paid him and we were headed for the door when he called to her.

"Hey Miss Lucy," he chuckled and leaned across the counter on his elbow.

"You picked up any ghosts, lately?"

"Not lately, Kaiser." Lucy said solemnly over her shoulder. She loaded the Jeep and we started back down the road. Reaching under the dash she yanked down quickly and the cap popped off a cold R.C. Cola. She handed it to me, along with a chocolate Butterfinger.

"Peace offering, okay?" She said, and I nodded my head but didn't speak.

"There was a good reason I never stopped for that old woman." Lucy was silent for a moment and I saw her let out a deep breath like she might have been holding it in for a long time.

"But why didn't you stop Lucy, she was all alone out there."

"Because, I picked her up once before,.
She was walking in the fog before tonight?"

35

Her voice dropped until I could barely hear her. "She walks all over these hills, Jo Jo, you see, she's a ghost." My Butterfinger stuck in my throat.

"People around here say she's walked these hills for the past hundred years. I didn't know about her, and I picked her up about five miles from here one night".

"I felt sorry for her, thought she was somebody's Mother, you know? I had the truck then and I walked back down the road to get her."

"When I helped her get in on the passenger side. . ." Lucy closed her eyes and shuddered. "I could feel her thin bones under the shawl; it was like she was made of sticks or something. I ran around to my side of the truck, and she was gone. I was on a narrow dirt road with open fields on both sides, and she'd vanished into thin air. I looked up and down that road for half an hour and didn't find a trace of her."

We were both quiet as she drove up the steep side of the mountain, each of us in our own thoughts. When we turned onto the five mile road that was the lane to Lucy's farm though, she reached across the seat and tapped me on the arm.

"Now do you see why I'm so scart?" I shrugged my shoulders, I could relate to her fear of the dark and her imagination that the old lady was a ghost; after all I grew up with a houseful of roaming spirits. But I knew for sure that the old lady wasn't a ghost, I'd seen her up close when we passed her on the mountain and she was as real as Lucy.

I didn't know the answer, but I did know the question. Why was the old lady walking in the hills in the first place? And why at night, in the fog?

I smiled, maybe she was looking for her cat. Or maybe she was crazy. Anything was possible, except that she was a ghost, and I knew for sure that she wasn't.

I had to laugh when I thought about how much alike Lucy and Earl was in their fear of the unknown. Earl was just as convinced he might encounter a spook, as Lucy was that she actually saw one. At that moment I felt pretty smart for an eight year old girl, but then I had grown up with Maw and mother and both of them always told it like it was, come hell or high water.

Just then I felt Lucy brake and slow down, there was something ahead of us in the glare of the headlights, but it was difficult to see in the fog.

"What is it Lucy?" I could just make out a spot of brown now and then as the mist lifted.

"Don't know for sure, it could be a deer or one of our cows got loose."

We were driving real slow and I leaned out the side of the Jeep, I wanted to get a good look at it. Lucy reached over and pulled me back against the seat, knocking the wind out of my chest as she slammed down hard on the gas. We lunged forward and I found myself clinging to her shirt sleeve as we flew past the object in the fog.

It was like everything was in slow motion. I twisted my head around, frame by frame, and blinked my eyes. Incredibly, there was the old woman. She was bent miserably over her cane, shuffling along the road, eight miles from where we had last seen her. She turned and threw her hand up as we passed and then she was gone, sucked back into the folds of the fog.

I glanced at Lucy and she reached over and patted my head, "I told you the truth, didn't I, Jo Jo?" Her voice wavered and I knew how scared she was.

I nodded my head but I couldn't answer, my own voice was gone and it occurred to me that maybe I wasn't the smarty pants that I thought I was. Maybe I didn't know the question after all, let alone the answer.

{Sunday School lesson # 29: "Judge not, least ye be judged."}

The Green Bike

It was Saturday and I had gone downtown with Dad to pay his Monkey Wards bill. It was early March and snowing; my bare legs were cold and I wished I had not insisted on wearing my Mary Jane's and ankle stockings but I was a stubborn eight year old and bound to learn things the hard way. We had stopped to visit with Grandma Tippy Toe, she had made lunch, and we listened to the Gospel Hour. It was after we left her that I saw the green bike in the window of the hardware store. It was Chartreuse, a new color that year, the brightest green I had ever seen, and I pressed my face against the glass to get a better look.

It had a white leather seat and white leather streamers hanging from the handlebars. The back extended to carry a friend, and the wide panel down the front had a silver button on it for the horn. A large chrome light was mounted on the front to complete the beauty of its lines.

"That is the most beautiful bike I've ever seen." I whispered.

"That sure is a pretty shade of green, all right." Dad came over and breathed on the glass with me.

"Come on Snake, let's go in and look her over," he used that old nickname on me and it made me laugh, but I shook my head.

"No, we might miss our bus. We better not," I said. I knew we couldn't afford it, and I didn't want to see it and touch it and know that some other kid would be riding it. He took my hand and pulled me into the store. My legs felt stiff and my heart was pounding in my ears.

He ran his fingers over the chrome fenders, feeling for imperfections. When he could find none, he looked up at me and grinned.

"Good chrome job on there, baby."

He should know, he was one of the best electroplaters in the state.

But times were hard, and the plant had cut his work to the bone. We were eating beans and potatoes with a mix of mustard greens just to keep all of us kids regular, mother said.

When the salesman came over, I pulled on dad's sleeve to leave. I could see how the guy was looking us over. A man in a scarred leather jacket and jeans; a little girl in a gray coat. I was surprised when he smiled.

"You like this bike young lady?"

I nodded my head and stared hard at my shoe laces.

"This is a nice bike," dad was still looking it over, "how much are you asking for it?"

"This is a new model out this year. It sells for $25.98."

Dad looked at me and then at the salesman. "I've got real good credit in this town. Do you think I could get this bike on time?" he asked.

They left and went into the back office while I touched every inch of the bike with my index finger and smelled the leather on the seat and handlebar streamers.

When they came out of the office they were smiling. The salesman kicked the bike stand up, and leaned the handlebars towards me. I felt hot all over, I couldn't breathe.

I hugged my father and cried until the front of his shirt was wet.

"Hey, I thought you'd be happy." He grinned down at me.

"I am," I sniffed, "but how will we get it home?"

"Well, the snow is melting so you can ride and I'll walk. It won't be so far. Besides, we have the bike to look at all the way home, don't we?"

I could see the light in his eyes and I realized that the green bike was as much for him as it was for me. I thought that it had somehow restored his pride in his own ability to provide, in a time when his self esteem was at its lowest point. By the same token I realized, if he had not been able to buy the bike, it could have broken his spirit.

What did it matter if we didn't have a car, or meat in the house, or enough milk. We could eat beans and potatoes; a man's pride is not measured in the fullness of his belly. It was a lot of wisdom for an eight year old to digest, but I understood it fully as we walked into the setting sun and through the back gate to the house where mother was waiting with her arms folded.

"A new bicycle?" She frowned hard at dad, "How could you buy a bicycle when we can't afford a damned chicken to put in the pot!" I was next on her list, "And how could YOU talk your father into doing something that stupid, Jo?"

I hunched my shoulders and studied the worn pattern on the throw rug. A tear squeaked out of the corner of my eye, and landed on the toe of my shoe. The ache in my throat was too big to swallow.

Maw, the old Rebel, sat glaring at me over her silver rimmed glasses. "You'll be wishin' you had a bite of bread, instead of that ridin' cart, mark my words, girl."

"Hey now, it wasn't her fault," Dad sat down and lit a Lucky Strike. "I wanted to get the bike, and I did. That man down at the hardware store said I had the best credit he'd ever seen, told me I could have anything in the damn store if I wanted it."

"Too bad they wasn't selling FOOD!" Mother threw back as she left the room.

Three days later I went out on the back porch to get the bike, and it was gone. I scoured the neighborhood and no-one had seen it. Ralph Littler, one of the redheaded kids that lived over on River Street in back of our house, told me he had seen my brother Jerry with a beautiful green bike going up the embankment to the railroad tracks. I ran like the wind and I found him, but I was too late.

He was already racing down the embankment, chunks of gravel and black dirt striking the sides of the bike. He landed in the street with the bike overturned and the beautiful panel dented.

That night when dad came down the alley carrying his lunch bucket I thought he would whip Jerry until he cried, but he didn't. Instead he looked at me and shook his head.

"That was your fault," he said to me. "You didn't take care of it. That was your job, to take care of that bike. Now it's a piece of damn trash."

My heart cracked down the middle but I knew he was right. I filled a bucket with warm water and soap and I went out and cleaned the railroad dirt from the beautiful green metal and scoured the seat and tires nearly white again. That winter the dents rusted and the bike ended up in the basement. From that moment on, I hid everything, like a little mouse, as soon as it came into my possession. As a matter of fact, I still do.

The Equinox

When I was eight years old my father was laid off from his job for two months and he was finding it difficult to bring home enough money to keep us all fed and pay the bills. In all the years of my life I had never seen him miss a day of work or ever be late, even when he had to take the bus in the worst snowstorm known to man. Now he was finding odd jobs here and there until the factory called him back.

We never went hungry, there was always something hot on the table, but we were eating a lot of potatoes and eggs.

It was spring, and the snow had been melting into messy puddles all week while the trees were bumpy with the promise of blossoms. But on this Saturday morning it was bitter cold and ice edged snow blew like tiny pellets against the front window of our house.

"It's the equinox," Maw said when she saw the snow storm. "What's an equinox?" I asked her.

"That's when the sun crosses the equator and it makes the day and the night everywhere, of equal length. This here is March the 20th, so this is the Vernal equinox. They'll be another one in the fall around about September 22nd, if I recollect, and that one, now let me see...that one'd be called the Autumnal equinox. They can cause the weather to be ornery for a spell."

I stood looking at her. Maw never ceased to amaze me, just when I thought she didn't know anything, except about the Civil War, she started sounding like a Professor.

"Ruth, are you sure you want to make this trip, its awful cold out there, girl." Maw pulled the curtain back to look at the snow.

"Jo just got over the croup and she needs to stay here where it's warm."

"We'll be fine, mommy, now I need to go before Clyde gets home."

Mother bundled me into my Eskimo coat with the fur rimmed collar and pulled wool leggings on me, zipping up the sides. I found my red gloves with the hole in the thumb and we set out to walk the 20 blocks to Mattie's house on Sullivan Avenue. I didn't have to whine and beg to go this time; mother wanted me along for support I think, or sympathy.

Mattie was my father's oldest sister and she owned a small apartment building downtown. She operated a beauty salon in the basement that was accessed by a side entrance from the street. Steps led down to a glass front door with a small window at the side where a blue neon sign flashed, "Beauty Shop" across the ankles of passing pedestrians on the sidewalk.

This was where I lost all my hair and dignity every Saturday before Easter. Mattie wired my hair into metal rods, and saturated it with a solution that smelled like skunk urine. Then she stuck me under a huge machine, and turned on the heat, like some mad scientist I thought, until my head began to feel scorched. She would leave the tiny shop and go upstairs to her main floor apartment for lunch while I jerked and twisted like an eight year old on death row.

When I was done cooking she shampooed my hair and set it in pin curls against my fried scalp and stuck me under a scorching dryer for 40 minutes. It was her Easter gift to me. Then I was brushed and combed into the exact hairdo of Joan Crawford.

The next morning, Easter Sunday, I would go to church smelling like a dead skunk from the permanent wave solution, and by then my hair was a huge ball of fuzz. From then until late summer I looked like Orphan Annie.

That Saturday morning mother and I managed to walk the ten freezing blocks from our house to High Street, where at least we could stop in the lobbies of the big office buildings downtown and press into the wall heaters to try and get warm before going the next 10 blocks to Livingston Avenue.

My toes were numb, her face was pink from the cold, and the hole in my shoe kept sucking my sock out of it. Every other block I had to take off the shoe and pull the wet sock back in.

Dad had an account at Montgomery Wards and twice a year he and mother took all of us kids there for Christmas toys and school clothes. He always bought me Spaldings, the best shoes money could buy he said, and every Spring I would have a hole in the soles as big as a quarter. Finally, he sent me to Tony's Shoe Repair on Broad Street to have cleats put on the soles.

Tony sat on his little wooden stool with his mouth rimmed with shoe tacks. I was fascinated as he spit them out like a machine gun and nailed them to the shoe soles. His front tooth showed gun metal gray and the tip of his tongue was black from the nails.

The cleats he put on my heels and toes were huge, because he was out of the small ones, he said. They helped to save my shoes that following winter but you could hear me walking five blocks away.

When mother and I finally arrived at Mattie's building we went down the wrought iron steps into her beauty shop where the smell, of permanent wave solution was strong as cow piss. Mattie was a good hairdresser and she had a big clientele. She was combing a sticky light colored liquid that looked like snot into a lady's hair and arranging it into perfect waves. She clamped each wave tight to her head with little jaw-like clips before putting her under a hot dryer. When she finished she took us briskly upstairs to her suite of apartments and turned to mother.

"What could possibly have brought you out in this awful storm, Ruth?"

Mother's head dipped and I saw her swallow her pride.

"For Gods sake Ruth, nothing has happened to Clyde, has it?" Mattie stepped forward and clutched the back of the dining room chair. "Or Herb"?

Mother shook her head, but she didn't look up for a moment. When she spoke it was slowly as if each word was in capital letters and stuck in her throat.

"Mattie, I hate to ask… and you know I never have before." She twisted her gloves and jammed them into her coat pocket.

"But I was wondering, if you could see your way clear, to let me borrow eight dollars. It's just until mommy gets her pension check next Friday."

She was biting her lower lip, and I saw what it was costing her to ask. There was a stretch of silence when I could hear the great chiming clock in the hall shift gears and slowly strike the hour. The peal of the chimes striking ten rose to the top of the 16 foot ceilings and echoed throughout the house like a Sunday morning prayer meeting.

I had time to study the picture of Jesus, with his eyes that magically opened. The pupils were faintly painted on his closed lids and if you squinted at him intently enough, the eyes seemed to pop open. They popped open now, and stared at me accusingly, while I squirmed inside my hot coat. When Mattie finally spoke I jumped. "Ruth," she folded her arms and leaned against the cherry breakfront by the marble fireplace. "As much as you hate to ask, that is how much I hate to refuse you."

Mother stared at nothing; she was as silent as the snow flakes piling on the window ledge outside. Mattie glanced at her watch. "I don't feel like I would be doing you a favor Ruth, if I gave you the money. Oh it isn't that I don't have it, of course I do, but you and Clyde have a family, and I think you need to be aware of that fact in the future. If I were to loan you money now, you wouldn't have learned a darn thing about responsibility. Can you see what I mean?"

Mother remained silent. Mattie walked toward the kitchen looking at her watch.

"I have someone under the dryer, but I can make you a quick cup of hot tea and give you a ticket for the bus." Mattie clucked her tongue, "You both look nearly frozen to death."

Mother tilted her chin and I saw the strong Virginia pride that Maw displayed so often. She pulled thin gloves out of her coat pocket; they were still wet on the fingers. She buttoned my Eskimo hood tight to nearly choking, around my neck, and pulled me after her to the door. Mattie turned her palms up and walked quickly after us.

"Aren't you staying for the tea?" Her eyebrows arched and she looked surprised.

Mother shook her head, "No, we have to be getting home now." We stepped out the door into the white blizzard and suddenly she stopped and looked back at Mattie standing in the doorway. "But thanks anyway, Mattie." she said.

"Well at least take the bus tickets, Ruth." Mattie called out over the wind.

"We walked here Mattie, and we can walk back." I was so proud of her that I had a lump in my throat I couldn't swallow, and so awful cold by the time we finally got home that I nearly threw up.

Dad was there when we walked in. Mattie had called to see if we had made it home all right, she was worried he said, and felt bad about not loaning mother the money she had asked for. He was Indian crazy when he found out she had gone to his sister with our personal problems. His pride was shattered and so was the coffee cup he had been drinking from.

"Look Clyde, I made a mistake, okay?" Her eyes glistened and tears trembled against her lashes. "But I can guarantee you one thing; I won't ask anyone for money again, not as long as I draw a breath on this earth." And she never did.

When the Ghost Walks

On the first of every month Maw tore out to the mailbox to get her pension check. Everything hinged on her check. It meant she could ride the bus downtown and browse all afternoon in the stores, have lunch at Kresges and take in a matinee at the Avondale. And she could buy sweet rolls, her passion food.

"You've been out front twice this morning mommy, and you know the mailman don't come till noon." Mother spit on her iron to see if it was hot and passed it over a white pillowcase.

"I was wantin' to go downtown and see Clark Gable before it got too hot today." Maw took clothes from the laundry basket and sprinkled them with water from a bottle. Then she rolled them tight and placed them in another basket for mother to iron.

"Clark Gable is downtown?" Mother asked her.

"It's that picture show, "Gone With The Wind." I read about it in the Dispatch, it's a story about how the North come and stole our land. It'll cost me dear to see it at the RKO Palace, but I wouldn't miss Clark Gable if I had to pay a dollar to get in.

"There goes the mailman now, he's early." Mother told her, and Maw banged out the screen door. A moment later she came back with a smile on her face.

"I got my check, the ghost walked and the eagle shit." She untied her apron and headed upstairs to get dressed.

"Why does she say that stuff about the ghost, and the eagle?" I asked.

"It's just her way. See that eagle on her check?" Mother pointed and I saw the eagle with his wings spread and the words, USA under it.

"I think that's the eagle shit, but you'll have to ask her about the ghost." she said.

I wanted to go downtown with Maw, sometimes she took me, and we had fun. Except for the times she got a dirty fork or spoon at the lunch counter in Kresges, and then I wished I was invisible.

"You! Girlie!" she' shouted, "Come over here for just a minute." Maw held the fork high over her head like a torch on the statute of Liberty as the waitress waited to hear her complaint. "I might be a poor old woman, but I'll be damned if I'll eat with something that's been halfway down another person's gullet, AND STILL HAS THE FOOD LEFT ON IT."

I watched as every person at the crowded lunch counter stopped eating and carefully examined their forks,

"I'll get you another fork right away, Missus," and the pale faced waitress brought her a clean fork. Maw adjusted her glasses and examined the fork, holding it up against the ceiling lights and peering into each curved tong, then wiped it thoroughly with her napkin.

"Now this one is CLEAN." she announced, and a sigh of relief rippled down the lunch counter as everyone continued eating.

One time Maw took my younger brother Jerry, downtown with her to shop, I say "one time" because that was the end of it, he was notorious for doing something outrageous. One time, he poured a mound of salt on a man's pie sitting next to him in a diner when the poor guy had looked away for a moment. Then while Maw was looking at girdles in the Boston store he pretended to have an epileptic fit on the floor.

The sales clerk wanted to call the emergency squad but Maw wouldn't let her.

"But he's having a fit!" The girl screamed, "We have to do *something*, he could die!"

"Trust me, he won't die till I get him home," While Jerry thumped and gagged on the floor, Maw stepped over him and walked out the door. The horrified clerk ran after her.

"Are you just going to *leave* him?" she screeched.

"Tell that idiot, when he gets done doin' his floor dance, that I went home." And she did.

Maw came downstairs wearing her navy dress with the big white flowers on it and her black hat with the pearl pin in the front. She stuffed white gloves in her purse along with the pension check and headed for the door.

"Can I go?" I ran after her like a puppy.

"You ain't ready, and I don't want to miss Clark Gable. Besides, you got us thrown out of the Avondale last time, because you was kicking the seat in front of you."

"I had to pee," I said lamely.

"That ain't the truth and you know it. When you can sit still without your hands between your legs, long enough for me to see an entire picture show, then maybe I'll take you, but not today. Go help your mother, dampen and fold that laundry for her. I didn't suffer death to give her life, so she could wait on you children hand and foot."

I thought it served her right that she went to the wrong theater. After standing in line for thirty five minutes, she saw Errol Flynn when the curtain went up. Tearing down the dark aisle she grabbed a young usher by the arm dragging him after her to the lobby.

"Clark Gable ain't in this picture at tall. This, she shouted, is that skirt sniffing drunk, Errol Flynn. He can't hold a candle to Clark. By God, I want my money back, and I want it now."

"You're the third old lady in ten minutes that came to the wrong theater." he sighed. "Gable's over at the LOWE'S, across the street."

Mother was ready to call the police when Maw wasn't home by dark that night. We walked to Broad and Central and waited by the White Castle for the buses coming from downtown.

"Somebody could have robbed Mommy, and killed her for that pension check." Mother wrung her hands as she watched for yet another bus.

It was difficult for me to see anyone robbing Maw. Her family survived Bulls Run and she had their blood racing through her veins. If anyone was in trouble, I thought it was probably the robber. She was on the fourth bus; she'd stayed and watched Gone With The Wind twice.

On the walk home she told us all about how Clark Gable had locked bills with Vivian Leigh, against her will, and how he had said, "Frankly my dear, I don't give a *damn."*

I thought I saw a flash of wishful thinking in Maw's eyes just then, like maybe she was remembering when she was eighteen, a pretty young girl with black hair to her waist, who had to borrow a white dress for the town dance, and became the belle of the ball. I realized that after all these years the pretty young girl still lived in her heart, waiting for her Clark Gable.

Those Damn Harris Boys

By the time I was 11 years old there were four boys in the family and a girl on the way. There was Jerry 10, Leroy 9, Earl 8, David 7, and Marilyn Rose, ready to make her entrance.

Maw loved the boys best, and barely tolerated me. I figured it was because they were always bringing something home for her, some little treasure they'd found on the tracks or down by the river, or if she was very lucky, off the dump.

One year the day after Christmas, Walter Dolder called Leroy aside and told him he could have all the trees left over in Dolder's Grocery Store lot. Because the trees were grossly overpriced like everything else in the store, there were a lot of them left.

Mother's sister, Pernoon, and her 16 year old son Harold, (aka Buddy) had just moved out of our house the month before. They had found a little three room apartment on the second floor of an old house on Hayden Avenue. There were 40 wooden steps attached to the outside of the house with a precarious railing that led to a tiny porch and, The door to Pernoon's apartment. That's where the boys stacked the Christmas trees. All 15 of them.

Harold couldn't get out of the house, Pernoon couldn't get in. No-one knew where the trees came from or who had put them on the porch. It was a dark mystery, until an eye witness to the deed, Pernoon's nosy next door neighbor, told how he himself had seen everything.

He said there were three boys, two of them tow headed, and the other one was skinny with dark hair and he talked very loud. One of them he said, he remembered real good, because he had yellow hair and weird eyebrows that came up into points in the middle.

"They were just a haulin' and a haulin' those trees up the steps." He declared. Suddenly Harold snapped his fingers, he knew who those tree haulers were, instantly. It was those damn Harris boys!

"I'm not going to stand still for any lying." Mother told the boys. "I want to know who took those Christmas trees, and why they were left on Pernoon's porch." She put her hands on her hips, "My sister has enough to contend with, and you boys know it. And I don't want to hear any lies about it either. I better NOT hear any damn lies."

"You can lock up a thief and throw away the key, but you can't lock up a liar's tongue." Maw said, she had a motto for every evil deed known to man.

"Awkkkk!" Leroy hollered, it was a strange name the boys had attached to Mother, and it sounded like the screeching of a prehistoric bird, especially if they were excited when they called her name, and Leroy usually was. I covered my ears, his loud voice could be heard for miles when he was upset, he took it after the Johnson's side of the family, mother decided. She said you could hear them whispering all the way down to Broad Street, eight blocks from our house.

"AWKKK, WALTER DOLDER GAVE US THOSE TREES." Leroy exploded.

"I don't care if God almighty gave them to you. I'm going to Amlin with Zeta to get eggs from the Amish, and when I return, I want all those damn trees taken right straight back," she pointed her finger in the air, "where ever they came from."

That night as soon as it was dusk there was hurried shadows on Harold and Pernoon's porch and the next morning the trees were gone.

They were returned to Dolder's lot, but Earl was caught carrying a tree by Norman, Walter's brother. Walter hadn't told Norman about the tree deal he had made with Leroy, and Norman thought Earl was stealing.

"You should be ashamed. I should call up your mother and tell her, that her son is a THIEF!"

"I'm bringing the goddamn tree *back!* I'm not *stealing* it."

Earl was 8 years old with buttercup blonde hair that lay around his head in a mass of curls and soft blue eyes. He looked angelic, but he had a mouth that could make a nun faint. When he was angry or frustrated he cussed, it was his defense against the kids at school. Children can be savage as man eating tigers if their classmates show any deviation from the standard and Earl had a speech defect that made it difficult for him to pronounce words.

When they were cruel, Earl learned to lash back with a cuss word that sent them reeling. The more effective it was, the more cuss words were added the next time around. He was careful not to cuss around mother and dad or Maw, though. She called him her "Little angel boy."

"Earl is as clever as a pocket in a shirt." Maw told a distant cousin who had stopped by the house one summer to stay for a week, unannounced. When he came down to breakfast one morning and found that Earl had dismantled his expensive watch, he exploded.

"I bought that watch in London!" His voice cracked, "it cost me a damn fortune."

"I scolded him for taking it apart." Mother was cracking eggs into her big iron skillet. "I think when he saw it laying on the parlor floor where you dropped it last night when you was dead drunk, well I think his curiosity just got the better half of him."

Mother didn't like the idea that cousin Emmit had decided to just drop in, and proceed to lay drunk for two days, even if he was from the money side of the family. And Maw didn't like him at all. She thought he was a thief and a liar.

"I don't care if his mother does have money, he's still a damn thief," Maw declared. "He'd steal Christ from the cross, and go back for the nails."

I thought if Aunt Net or Uncle John from the Valley View Church of Christ in Christian Union where I went to Sunday school ever heard her say that, they'd both drop dead in their tracks. Mother had that quirky look on her face while she poured the coffee and I knew she was pulling Emmit's chain.

"Now if that was *my* watch," she sighed, "I'd just let Earl put it back together again." When Earl handed him the watch after breakfast, it was in perfect running order. But I knew it would be. Earl always untangled the hopeless knots out of my necklaces, and patiently extracted the tiniest splinter from a finger, with the expertise of a master surgeon.

Jerry on the other hand, was the thoughtful one, but he was always getting into some weird kind of mischief. Nothing big, just little things, that drove my father crazy. Jerry was born an adult. From the time he was four he drank coffee and poured it into his saucer just like Maw, sipping it out with a long sucking sound.

He liked to study people's actions and he could mimic them like a trained actor. He was forever exploring new and exciting territory for more material and he found a treasure trough just four miles from our house, at the State Hospital. There were two facilities, one for the mentally retarded, the Hospital; and one for the criminally insane, the Asylum. This facility was for the Lizzie Bordens and Charles Mansons.

The State farmed about 15 acres surrounding the State Hospital grounds and let the less violent patients work in the fields as a kind of therapy. When Jerry was nine years old he walked the railroad tracks to the State Hospital, slid down the embankment and walked into the work fields to mingle with the patients.

After he had been sneaking into the fields for three weeks he knew most of the patients by their first names and they welcomed him. He hung out, helped them pick vegetables and shared his experiment ideas with them. When the whistle blew at noon and the patients lined up for lunch Jerry went with them into the cafeteria.

One day he was in the lunch line when the nurses were handing out little green pills to the patients.

When they came to Jerry in the line they thought he was a midget.

They soon discovered he wasn't a patient and they called mother to come and get him, immediately. The hospital was furious and Jerry was warned to stay off the grounds. They told him he would go to the juvenile detention hall three buildings down on West Broad Street if he ever dared to come back.

"I don't want to EVER catch you on these hospital grounds again, kid." The beefy security guard at the main entrance warned Jerry. "If I catch you, you'll be sorry, you understand me?"

"I understand." Jerry looked sincere, but I saw the corners of his mouth twitching when he added, "you won't catch me on the hospital grounds again."

And the guard never did catch him because he was careful, but Jerry was his own worst enemy. One hot summer day mother and Maw were in the back yard hanging up the laundry when he came through the gate with two men following on his heels.

"Who in the name of God, is *that*?" mother said.

"It beats me, but they must be from the Harris side, nobody looks like that in my family." Maw put her clothespins back in the sack and turned to greet the visitors.

It was mid August and the temperature was wavering between 85 and 90, yet one of the men with Jerry wore a red wool cap perched on top of his head and a long black coat buttoned tight to his neck. He looked to be about 7 feet tall with his long arms and dangling fingers nearly touching his knees. A purple scar on his right cheek took a sharp turn and ended under his left nostril.

The other man was small as a seven year old child, with a sharply narrowed face like an angel fish, and long baby fine blonde hair. He was in constant motion, leaping wildly around the yard with his arms held over his head. His brown knit shirt and matching pants making him look like a huge moth beating its wings against a lighted window pane.

Jerry was delighted, showing all of his teeth both top and bottom while he introduced his new friends to mother, who stood glaring at him with her arms folded.

"Awk," Jerry whispered with his hands held together, "this is Professor Golden, from the State Hospital." The big man nodded and mother nodded back. "And this," Jerry tried to grab hold of the moth man without any success. "And that, was Charles." he said.

"Say hello to Awk, Charles." Charles threw his head back and crowed, "Helloooo, Awwwwk, hellllooooo Awwwwwwwkkkkkkkkk."

"Jerry," mother grated, "you shouldn't have taken them away from the hospital."

Maw wagged her finger at Jerry. "You knew better than to go on the State Hospital grounds, you were already warned about that, weren't you."

"I believe it is quite explanatory, in my view." Professor Golden said as he thoughtfully fingered the scar on his face. Maw and mother looked at him, both of them speechless.

"You see," he paused to ponder with his arms tightly folded, "during my acquaintance with the adolescent, I have concluded that he is uniquely inquisitive about everything in his environment. I find him to be quite the little genius, I must say."

Mother wasn't sure she agreed with that theory and told the professor so, and they ended by having a 35 minute debate on the subject of genius, versus the need for attention or a good ass switching, compliments of the lilac bush.

"If he goes back to that State Hospital again, I'll give him enough attention to make his ass red." Mother told the professor.

She made lemonade, (Jerry told her that Maw's strong coffee would make them crazy,) and brought out a platter of warm biscuits that she and Maw had made that morning. She spread them with Amish butter and strawberry jam.

Professor Golden was delighted as he and Maw sat on the back porch and talked about the Civil war and the present state of the union.

Finally, mother called the hospital and told them what had happened. They sent three orderlies and a van to pick up Professor Golden and Charles. They also issued a strict warning to Jerry never to trespass again or he would be severely fined. It scared him so bad; he didn't go back for a month.

Jerry eventually lost interest in exploring the State hospital grounds and concentrated on his chemistry, especially after seeing Frankenstein plugged into lightning bolts and brought back to life at the Avondale Theater. It wasn't long until he started haunting the alleys after school looking for anything to help in his "experiments."

One night he came home with an armload of long glass tubes, rubber hoses and pieces of wire. He rushed upstairs to the room he shared with Leroy and Earl and closed the door. I knew what he was doing because he had told me, he was assembling his "machine."

However, since Jerry was notorious for nearly blowing up the house a few times with his experiments, Dad was close on his heels. The room was full of tall tubes and wires, coils and rubber hoses, foam pads and a strange device made of leather that looked like a huge belt.

"Where did you get all this stuff?" Dad frowned, picking through the debris.

"Clyde," Jerry twisted a wire around a piece of metal with a pair of pliers while he spoke, "I found all this stuff in back of the funeral home on Broad Street and I brought it home in my wagon."

Dad's fingers shot out like stars, and he screamed until I could see his tonsils.

"RUTHHHHHHHHHH!"

Mother dropped the plate she was drying and raced up the steps. "My God! What happened?" She looked at me and I shook my head, I thought he had lost his mind.

Dad was backed into the corner of the room with his hands flared out in front of him.

"He brought all that germy shit in here from the *funeral home.*" His eye balls rolled back in his head, "Those tubes! They still have blood stains in the bottom!" Dad had a long history of being a little germ crazy. "Get rid of it NOW!" He yelled.

Mother's fist rested on her right hip, it was apparent *she* wasn't going to touch it. "What do you expect *me* to do with it? Jerry needs to get rid of it, he brought it in here."

"I'll give you," Dad's finger shook as he pointed at Jerry. "I'll give you five minutes to get this stuff out of here, and back where you found it!"

"Clyde I can't! What about my experiment?" Whatever he had planned I knew he could do it. I had seen him make a blue arc dance between two rods as he blew up my bridal doll, so I knew he was serious about his experiment, whatever it was.

Dad's eyelids lowered into two gleaming slits as they swept the room and rested on Jerry's sincere face. "What in the hell ...are you going....to experiment *on*?"

"On *Miffy!*" Jerry's voice faltered and he drove his hands into his hip pockets.

"The CAT?" Dad's voice rose, "The one that got run over by a dump truck last week?"

"I know I can bring her back to life, Clyde. They did it to Frankenstein." There were tears in his eyes and mother went over to pat him on the head. She was ready to cry too.

"Jerry honey, even if you could, it would be cruel to bring her back." she told him, "Miffy is flat as a piece of cardboard, honey."

The corners of her mouth were twitching even though she still had tears in her eyes and so were mine.

We both fought hard to hold on for Jerry's sake, but when she asked him how he thought Miffy could possibly walk, even if he managed to bring her back.

I couldn't hold it in. I shrieked and fell against the door while tears ran down my cheeks and mother laughed so hard she had to bend over to hold her stomach.

"What in the hell, is going on up there?" Maw called up the steps.

When I told her, she beat her cane on the floor and laughed until I could see her gums.

All the tubes and hoses went back to the funeral home that very night and Jerry was sterilized with a scalding bath, sitting in the wash tub with his arms firmly folded. He was angry and humiliated. The next day he retaliated.

He went to see old Mr. Knapple, the drunken barber on Central Avenue where he had his head shaved, except for a thin ring of hair around his skull, like a balding old man. Mother. shook her head and dad was furious, but Mrs. Long, his third grade teacher called mother the next day.

"Mrs. Harris?" She said in her crisp voice, "I am afraid that Jerry is very disruptive to my class. The other children are laughing at him constantly and I must say, it is quite unnerving for me to see him sitting there with that bald head."

"I don't know what you expect me to do," Mother told her wearily, "I suppose I could paint hair on his head, or have him wear a cowboy hat to school." Mrs. Long never called again.

Dad was wild with rage; he knew that spanking was useless with Jerry. He decided to take his bike and put it in the basement for the summer and ground him, but before he could punish him, something happened, something absolutely terrible.

Jerry had sneaked out and spent the day at Bender's, a swimming pool on the hilltop. It was 91 degrees that day and I noticed that by late afternoon his bald head had turned red, and then purple, and it was beginning to swell *really really* big.

He was doing clown dives from the medium platform and as his head grew it looked like a beach ball, but it was soft as dough.

The dives started making his head look lopsided and all the kids laughed and poked their fingers in it, making little dents all over his purple head.

At first Jerry loved the attention, he was having fun. I tried to make him leave but he wouldn't, and after a while he started feeling dizzy and passed out. That was when we rushed him to the emergency room at Mt. Carmel. When he went in, the nurses gathered around and stared at him with their mouths open. He was a little boy with a huge purple lopsided head, full of blue veins and dents, rimmed in wild straw blonde hair. He looked like a space alien.

It was the first time I had ever seen him look scared. We were all scared as we sat huddled in the lobby of the hospital. It was nearly morning before he was out of danger and they kept him for three days while they packed his head in ice.

The swelling finally went down and we took him home. Everyone cried, we had nearly lost the little genius. After that episode he was strangely quiet for the rest of the summer.

Leroy was next in the womb after Jerry, lean and fine-boned he exuded innocence, but he was a co-conspirator in some of Jerry's most devious schemes. Earl was included in some of the mischief but David was still too little. He would make up for it when he got older, though.

Leroy looked fragile but it was a ruse. I discovered this aspect of his personality when he had saved some money selling pop bottles for a cowboy shirt at Danzigger's on Broad St. It cost three dollars, but Leroy never paid top dollar for anything if he could bargain.

"Will you take a dollar for that cowboy shirt in the window?" He asked Mr. Danzigger.

"A dollar?" Mr. Danzigger gargled, "What do you take me for anyhow, an idiot? That shirt is clearly marked for three dollars, you should learn to read."

"It's been in the window for a month and it's starting to fade from the sun. Pretty soon nobody will want it. What do you say, a buck?"

Danzigger pulled on his chin and went to the front window to look at the shirt. "I can let you have it for maybe two dollars, and not a nickel less."

"I'll have to think about it. Two dollars is the best you can do?"

"You want I should go broke and have to close my store or something?" Leroy walked out. Danzigger threw his arms up and ran after him. "Do you want the shirt or what?"

Leroy handed him the dollar and two quarters and took the shirt. It was what he had wanted to pay for it anyway. He kept the shirt buttoned to the neck on a hanger in his closet. He was waiting for a special occasion to wear it. A month went by and it hung in the closet until one Monday morning he came screaming down the steps to the kitchen.

"Where's Jerry!" He shouted in his Johnson's voice. Maw was turning pancakes over in the flat bottomed skillet.

"He's already left, said he had a score to settle with the Gardeners." Maw wagged the pancake turner at Leroy, "you boys better not be a fightin.' Clyde'll take the hide off both your arss's."

Mother was forcing me to walk Jerry to school because the Friday before, he'd came home with another bloody nose, compliments of the Gardener boys. I was pretty sure they wouldn't mess with me, I was older and I was a girl. Not that hitting a girl ever stopped a West Side boy, I knew that for a fact and I had the scars to prove it.

Besides, they didn't want the "mark of the ruby," from my square cut ring, on their face, like some of the other boys at school that I had fought with. I could give as good as I got, it was a lesson you learned early on the West Side, or you didn't survive the first grade. Plus I had to live up to Joe Louis, my namesake.

The three Gardener boys were standing on the corner when we turned to walk down Cable Avenue. They were all big stubby haired blondes with broad shoulders and missing teeth.

I knew they wouldn't try anything with Jerry when I was with him.

As we walked by they watched us under hooded eyes. My mouth went dry, the last thing I wanted to do was tangle with three boys when I was wearing my new Sunday school pin for perfect attendance. We were almost in the clear when incredibly; Jerry stopped and rolled his tongue out at them. I figured if they didn't beat him to death, I was going to.

I was so angry I kept walking, but Jerry didn't notice. By the time he realized that he was standing alone with his tongue hanging out on his chest, it was too late. They had him by the front of his shirt, or rather, Leroy's new cowboy shirt.

He didn't deserve it, but I knew I was going to have to save him. After all, we shared the same blood of our parents. I took off my Sunday school pin, dropped it in my coat pocket and started back to get Jerry. That was when I heard the blood curdling scream. It made the fine hairs on my arms stand up. Later in life I learned it was the same Rebel yell that sent chills down the spines of the Yankees during the Civil War.

I looked up and saw Leroy charging for the Gardeners like a raging bull. His little arms and legs were spinning around like windmills. He landed square into the center of the group, and the blood, spit and snot started flying. But it wasn't coming from Leroy; it was coming from the Gardener boys.

They had been hit by a sidewinder, a surprise attack, and they were still in shock. When the fighting was over and everybody swore revenge and pointed fingers at each other, Jerry thanked Leroy for saving his life.

"I didn't save you! I was saving my new shirt!" Leroy wiped his bloody nose on the back of his hand and shook his fist at Jerry. "You take my damn shirt off *right now* Jerry, and don't you *ever* touch it again!"

After that day, the Gardener boys made a wide path around Leroy Harris, and as word spread of his deed, he was revered by the underdogs and feared by the bullies all over the West Side and in New York City. Now *that* is the stuff that legends are made from.

Dolder's

Dolder's was a little market on Central Avenue, three blocks from our house. It was run by Norman Dolder and his brother Walter. There was a fresh meat counter, large produce section, four aisles of canned goods, and miscellaneous items in general. Walter was big and friendly with bushy dark hair and a quick smile for everyone. Mother liked him, and besides Dolder's was in the neighborhood.

When she was in the produce section Walter would smile and wag his finger at her when she nibbled on the fruit

"Now Ruth, that's a bad example for the children, you know."

Norman was nothing like his brother though, he was trim and dressed like a banker with stripped pants and a crisp shirt, silk vest and a bow tie. He slicked his hair back and sported a pencil thin mustache that rode his upper lip like a tiny black road.

His sharp eyes behind silver rimmed glasses scanned the store from his office on the second floor over the meat counter. Anyone he caught stealing or pulling pranks in the store was not allowed back in for rest of their lives. He stopped mother in the checkout line one morning.

"Ring her up for one peach, and a quarter pound of grapes." He told Edna, the nearly illiterate checkout girl.

"Where is them grapes and that one peach, Mr. Dolder?" Edna asked him.

"She ate the evidence!" Norman declared, "I saw her from my office, now do as I say and ring her up." Edna hesitated and chewed at the side of her lip. He pushed her aside and went back of the counter." Do I have to do everything myself?"

"You know that I have run a weekly tab in this store for the past three years Norman and I always pay it on Friday, regular as clock work."

Mother inched her face close to Norman's and her breath fogged his glasses when she spoke. "If you charge me for that peach and those little bit of grapes, I swear to God, I'll take my business over to Stoll's on Broad Street."

Walter came running down from the office and took Norman aside. "Are you out of your mind?" He whispered, "Ruth and Clyde Harris know everyone in the neighborhood. She could take half our business to Stoll's, if you persist in this pettiness."

Of course mother heard the entire conversation and when Norman turned a beaming smile to her, she threw her head back and turned away from him with her arms folded tight.

"Ruuuuth," he crooned, "I am sooo sorry. Of course, you don't owe me a dime."

She walked out of the store and left her groceries in the cart. Norman ran after her. "Where are you going? I said I was sorry, what do you want from me?"

"I'm going to Stoll's, and I want you to kiss my *ass*."

And he did. As word spread on the West Side about the "peach and grapes insult," nearly all of the neighborhood boycotted Dolder's and those that still went there, *hissed* at Norman. Two weeks later he came knocking on our door with a bag of peaches.

"Who's at the door, mommy?" Mother asked as she was frying fish for dinner.

"It's that little Jew, Norman Dolder, with a bag under his arm. Beware of Jews bearing gifts." Maw said.

"It's beware of Romans, mommy, but in this case I think you might be right, let him in. He took out a white handkerchief and dabbed at his forehead. He was still sweating as he set the bag on the table.

"Oh my, something smells good, is that fish?"

"It's cod. Stoll's gets it in fresh every Friday." Mother smiled wickedly.

"I love that Stoll's," Maw looked in the bag, "they got the best peaches in town."

"And cheap! Their prices are lower than anywhere else." Mother threw in.

"Don't pour that bit of grease out; we can add it to what's in the crock." Maw cautioned Mother.

"A woman can throw out more on a spoon, than a man can bring in with a shovel."

"That was good advice Mrs. Alwood, and quite true, my own mother would say the same thing," Norman beamed.

"I never saw a Jew yet, that would throw anything out." Maw told him.

"Well," Norman pulled on his tie, "I brought you a bag of peaches Ruth, I know how much you like them. Actually, it's a peach,..er... peace offering of sorts. We really value your business at Dolder's, you know."

"The only thing you value," Maw slapped the table with the palm of her hand, "is the God almighty dollar."

"But Ruth is a customer, and we consider her a valuable one."

"Bull*shit*!" Maw said. "If that girl standin' right there, was so valuable, then why did you chase her to the check out counter like she'd run off with one of them damn skinny chickens you overcharge everybody for?"

"Mommy!" Mother frowned, and then turned to Norman. "I might consider coming back to Dolder's if you was to do me a favor,"sweat poured off Norman's forehead,

"You ask me for a favor?" He pulled the white handkerchief out of his pocket again and wiped his face.

"What is it you want, Ruth?"

"I want you to let my boys back in the store."

Norman leaped off of the chair like someone had stuck a hot poker up his ass. He danced around the kitchen, jabbing his finger in the air, the little black mustache shrinking and expanding as his lips puckered and grew into a wide circle.

"That's impossible! You asked for too much, Ruth. Your son Jerry will slit open my fold overs and take all the cream out.

And that skinny one with the big eyes...."

"That'd be Leroy." Maw was setting the table for dinner.

"He's the one that put whip cream on that...that killer dog of yours, and let the beast loose in my store. It nearly caused a riot, everyone thought he had rabies. I could have been sued." Norman was hyperventilating. I got him a glass of water and he sat down, shaking.

"That dog was Prince, and he's gentle as a lamb, well unless provoked, and anyway, they never proved it was Leroy." Mother shook her finger at Norman.

"My boys are full of mischief, but I brought them up to be honest, and they don't dare lie to me." I nearly choked.

"And that little boy of yours," Norman puffed, "the one with the big head, he has got such a foul mouth. Foul! I heard him say the F word to my bag boy." The mustache made a figure eight as he sucked his lips into a bow.

Maw's head snapped around like a spring. "You mean that nigra you got working for you?"

"Now mommy, I like Carl and so do the boys. He carried a bag of potatoes home for Jo when she went to the store for me that time, and he didn't have to do it. Carl is a good boy."

"I never said you didn't like him, did I?" Maw bristled. "Next thing you know, you'll have him living with us."

"And another thing, your boys come in the store and get Carl to go fishing with them. He has a job to do, you know." Norman said.

"As I was saying," Mother ignored Maw and Norman, "If you don't want my boys in your store, I'll have to send them over to Murphy's when I need milk or bread."

"Now Ruth, you know perfectly well that Murphy is too high, he runs a small store and he can't buy in bulk like we do. Neither can Tom Darrow, his store is a hole in the wall, he is asking five times what we are, for eggs and milk."

Mother tapped her toe. There was a period of silence. Norman mopped his face and sighed. "All right, all right! The boys can come in the store *if* they behave."

After all the suffering Norman went through to get mother back, and all the things that Jerry did to drive him crazy, like putting the huge boxes of Kotex in the old women's grocery carts when they weren't looking, and walking through the store gargling and snarling with his arms jerking violently while pointing at the meat counter.

Then Norman did something that put dad on the warpath. He made me cry in front of the entire store.

Every Friday night Dad paid the grocery tab he ran at Dolder's for that week. He never missed a Friday, ever! Monday morning mother gave me a list of groceries and sent me to Dolder's. When I got to the checkout count, Norman stopped me.

"You can't have these groceries until your father pays his bill, young lady!"

"He paid the bill on Friday." I said, embarrassed because everyone in line was gawking at me, including Billy Hargrove, the love of my life, (at that particular moment.)

"Here is his bill, and as you can see, it was not paid!" Norman gave me the bill and it was not stamped with the three inch PAID IN FULL red stamp he always used. I didn't know what to do so I started wailing, showing all my bottom teeth, and ran out of the store. When I got home mother met me at the door.

"What happened to YOU?"

"Norman said dad never paid the bill, and he won't let us have any more credit until he does." I sobbed.

"WHAT?" said mother.

"WHAT?" said Maw?

That night when dad walked in the door from work, mother made me tell him exactly what had happened. When I got to the part where Norman made me cry in front of the whole store, I could see the war paint forming on his face. His eyes narrowed into blue sweeping lasers, and his jaw tightened.

"Come on!" He growled, "We have to go to the store, BABY!" He took my hand and race walked me to Dolder's, my hair standing straight out in the back.

Norman was behind the checkout counter with Edna and the store was packed. Dad stepped to the head of the line in front of an elderly woman with a hairnet riding over her eyebrows.

"Young man! How dare you try to dish me," her pruned lips folded into a pucker.

He turned around, and she saw what Custer must have seen in his final moments at Little Big Horn. The hidden warrior had emerged. She peeled rubber backing her cart out of his way as he reached across the counter toward Norman.

"This," Dad had a piece of paper clutched in his fist, "is my receipt, from Friday where I paid my bill, LIKE I ALWAYS DO!"

Norman blanched, the little black mustache hid under his nose.

"I don't do the bookkeeping Clyde, it was,....Edna, she does it."

"Then... you better get that bitch... some glasses, because my bill.... was PAID!" Dad was slow talking because his jaw was jutted way out to the side of his face.

Walter came running from the back of the store, his white butchers apron flapping between his legs and helped Norman find the bill. It hadn't been stamped. It wasn't paid.

"That's a damn LIE! I paid that bill myself." Dad said. "Now what are you going to do about it?" He was leaning across the counter with his fists in a knot.

People stood in line with ice cream dripping in their carts, cold milk was warming but no-one moved or made a sound. Babies sucked their thumbs silently and all eyes focused on my father.

"You knowww?" Edna said, rolling her eyes, "Now, that I think about it? Mr. Harris *did* pay that bill, cause I took the money."

"Then why didn't you STAMP IT?" Norman shouted.

"Maybe you stamped Hargrove's bill instead," I said, "they live on McKinley too."

Norman found Hargroves's bill and it was stamped, "Paid in Full." He called their house and asked if they had paid their bill last Friday. Mr. Hargrove had not paid the bill, but he would be in tomorrow, he said.

"What can I say, Cllllyde?" Norman mewed, "I am sooo *very* sorry you had to come down here to straighten this out, when it was Edna's fault."

"I'm not mad at her. It's YOU!" He grabbed Norman by the front of his shirt, and I thought he was going to faint.

"The hell with that BILL! Don't you EVER talk to my daughter like that again, or I'll come down here and stomp you like a cigarette butt!"

A&P opened a *Supermarket* downtown that summer, and dad bought a used car from his friend Gavoni. We never had to go to Dolder's again, except for milk and bread. And of course, mother always sent the boys.

Sisters

I have been accused of being a recluse, a lone wolf who peers out of her den for holidays, and only then, reluctantly. Perhaps it stems from the fact that our house was never empty when I was growing up there. Aside from my father's racing, boxing, guitar playing, beer drinking friends and brothers, there was mother's seven older sisters, five of which visited twice a week, and almost always for Sunday dinner.

There was Zeta, with her dark hair and lovely eyes who embraced her Spanish heritage with a passion, even though it was two generations past. She and her husband Floyd owned a restaurant on the hilltop and lived in the prestigious Valley View, in a house that smelled of cedar, lemon wax and rainbow cake with mile high frosting.

Sometimes she would take me home to play with my cousin Joan. It was Zeta who introduced me to fairies, toothpaste, and navel lint, for which I am forever grateful, especially the fairies, and most certainly the navel lint.

There was Nora, with her big bones and strawberry blonde hair showing streaks of gray. She told me endless tales of Lennie, her dead husband whom she worshipped. I felt like I had married him, I even knew the size of his boxer shorts. He had been dead for four years and she was still living with Zeta, she couldn't bear to be alone.

One summer Nora went to California to get her nose bobbed, but the surgeon botched the job horribly, and she ended up with a wad of flesh on her face. I never once heard her complain about it, I figured she was so full of misery and grief for Lennie that she had reached the saturation point for anymore heartache.

Cousin Joan and I sat on the back steps at Zeta's house, while Nora read from sheets of old poems she had collected. Most of them were about the Yukon. "A bunch of the boys were whooping it up at the Macmamell Saloon,and the kid that tickled the music box was playing a ragtime tune." I loved them, and as soon as I learned to write, I copied and read them every night.

There was Valice, with her short brown hair and smile that could light up a room. I was astounded at the number of teeth she had, they seemed to go all the way around her head. She had a voice that sounded as if it originated somewhere in her nasal cavities, and she liked to drag out her "N' words. She tended bar at Paul's Grill, a polite little establishment on Broad Street where they would throw you out if you farted, mother said.

I liked to stop in Paul's and visit with her on my way home from school. She would smile her, "Go home you little shit," smile at me, and give me a quarter. Because she was the midwife at my birth, mother had named me after her, and I hated it.

I was never called Valice though. Bernard, my cousin, was on the front porch with ten of dad's closest friends, listening to the radio as Joe Louis pounded Max Schmeling into unconsciousness.

I was born when Joe was pronounced, "Chaaaaaampion of the Woooorld," and Bernard christened me, "Jo, The Brown Bomber," with a drop of beer on my forehead.

The year that dad was put on part time at his job because there wasn't enough work, mother somehow managed to save a little money to buy Valice a small Christmas gift when she had come to have Sunday dinner with us.

"Oh Ruth, I didn't buy any gifts this year." Valice said, "But I did buy myself this new Chesterfield coat, I couldn't resist it. Being a widow, I don't have a man to support me like you do." She was a widow so many times that Jerry and I called her "The Spider Woman."

Aldie was next in line, a little chunky in the middle with her dyed black hair tied in a scarf around her head like a diaper and knotted in the front. She wanted to look like a Caribbean dancer, but I thought she looked more like the Mammy on the Log Cabin syrup tin. She had a bitter foul mouth, and Maw called her, "slew foot two," because she walked with her toes pointing out on either side, and one hand on her hip.

When I was eight years old she took me aside one day and told me that she knew our family talked about her, because she could hear them through her telephone, and I might just as well tell her everything they said. It sounded phony to me.

"If you can hear everything they say Aunt Aldie, then what can *I* tell you?"

She told me to go home.

Ethyl was the middle sister and she was my cousin Eva's Mother. I loved it when she came over on hot summer days and helped mother clean the house. She laughed and danced around the kitchen with the broom, her light brown hair wispy around her face.

When she walked, her head tilted to one side, a look of wonder on her face as if music played somewhere in the distance but she couldn't quite hear it. She was always smiling when I talked to her.

"Ethyl's awful tender." Maw would say. I never did figure out what she meant.

Mother, Maw and Ethyl, sat on the front porch drinking coffee and watching the lace curtains dry on the wooden racks, where they had them stretched out on tacks. The green blinds snapped and sucked against the windows in the early spring breeze, and Eva and I made mud pies in the side yard while the smell of Maw's light as a feather biscuits, filled the air as they baked.

Mother's oldest sister was Annie, but I called her Pernoon, and I loved her. She was my bar buddy. She was tall and thin and wore her dark curly hair to her shoulders even when the gray streaks threatened to take over.

In the Monkey's Nest and Mom Dago's Bar and Grill on Saturday nights, if she happened to be there, she danced with me until the wee hours, with her elbows poked out and her knees bent.

In the early morning after the bars closed, we sat in the back seat of my father's Plymouth on the way home, my eyes heavy with sleep while Pernoon cuddled me against her red fox stole, his dead eyes staring at me in the street lights. She smelled like vanilla and old books and I liked to rub the inside of her upper arm, it was soft as biscuit dough.

"Dammit, will you quit milking my arm? That skin is loose enough as it is, baby doll."

Last of all, there was Tady, the San Francisco belle, according to her. She owned a small apartment building in San Francisco. I saw her once, when she came to Columbus for a visit and stayed at our house. It was a huge mistake for everyone concerned, but especially for her.

I'd heard talk between the sisters about how mean Tady had treated Maw when she was living at home, before Tady started her bootlegging business and moved to Redwood City.

That was where she met her husband and bought the apartment building. Mother told me when she was 15 years old, that Valice and Tady came to the house with two men in fancy black suites and another blonde haired woman in a red dress with a big diamond on her finger.

"They were all dressed up like movie stars and arrived in a big black car. The woman went out to the privy and left her purse with the top open, lying on the table. Naturally I was curious so I glanced in the purse" mother said.

"Well, there was a wad of money with a rubber band around it that would choke a horse, and a small hand gun with a pearl handle. The girl let me hold the gun and gave me a dollar from the wad. Valice bragged that the guy and girl knew Dillinger and Pretty Boy Floyd."

The day that Tady stepped out of the taxi in front of our house, I saw a dark haired woman teetering on the brink of fat, but doing it in grand style. She wore an expensive looking gray stripped suit with a fur wrap and a felt hat cocked on the side of her head with black gloves and big pearl earrings.

"How ya doin' kiddo," she said, sounding like Mae West as she breezed past me on the front porch and I breathed in her spicy perfume.

She had the taxi driver carry in her red alligator luggage and she handed him a half dollar for a tip. He was so excited he tripped and fell off the porch. I was excited too, she was as close to a movie star as I had ever seen and I was fascinated. She sat down with mother and Maw in the front room and took a gold cigarette case out of her purse.

I" can't believe you still live here by the train yards, little sister." Tady produced a matching gold lighter and lit her cigarette, inhaling deeply and letting the smoke trail out through both nostrils. "Personally, I couldn't stand the filth."

Tady didn't like the train yards or the soot, but she took an immense liking to my father. That first night when she saw him coming up the back walk from work with his blue shirt open at the throat and his sleeves rolled to his elbows, she stiffened like a cheetah when it sees a white tailed deer. I watched her size him up and I knew she was ready for the chase.

"Now *that* makes the trip worth while," she said it very softly, but I heard her.

After dinner dad liked to sit in the parlor and listen to the news and read his paper. Tady sauntered in behind him though, leaving mother and Maw to do the dishes. She sat very close to him on the sofa and stared hard. Finally he put his paper down and asked her how she was.

"I'm good," she breathed, "I'm so damn good you wouldn't believe it if I told you, I'd have to show you." She said it in a husky voice, and when she laughed it sounded like a man.

"That's nice, I'm glad you feel good." He stood up abruptly, his mouth trying to figure out what to say. "Well," he folded his arms, "I had better go work on my bills now." He ran out of the room; I had never seen him act like that.

"I have to tell you Ruth, your husband is the best looking man I've seen in a long time." Tady sighed at breakfast the next morning. "If he wasn't already tied down I'd take him for myself. I bet I could teach him a thing or two." She laughed in her coffee cup.

Tady started giving dad a lot of attention, filling his cup with coffee when it was nearly empty, telling him how good looking he was, buying him imported beer and cigars.

At first mother thought it was funny, but he got to liking it. He stayed up later and later, long after mother went to bed, drinking beer and laughing with Tady until nearly midnight.

Jerry and I agreed that Tady was the woman in the song mother always sang to us. She was Christine Leroy, come to break up our happy home, such as it was.

I heard her singing it the next morning while she was hanging out the wash, her voice soft and sad in the morning air.

"Oh brother, I was only a dreaming, how happy our home was with joy,

Till that demon crept into our household, in the dark form of Christine Leroy.

How she came, with her face like an angel, to wish me a long life of joy,

A sight of such radiant beauty, in the beautiful Christine Leroy.

Oh, the time passed along and my husband, grew thoughtless and care worn each day,

And I knew it was the face of that demon, who heartlessly lured him away.

So at last one evening I found them, it seemed my whole life was destroyed,

Hand in hand with her head on his shoulder, stood my husband and Christine Leroy.

Oh, brother I'll never be better; it's useless in telling me so,

My poor heart lies waiting forever, for a resting place under the snow."

I had to sleep with Maw and Jerry, in her big soft bed since our "guest" had taken my room. I was worried and lay awake until the hall clock chimed 10:00, and mother come up the steps and closed the door to her room.

There was a hum of voices downstairs in the parlor, Dad's male voice and then Tady's grating laughter, but it was the periods of silence that I was worried about. And I decided I wanted a drink of water, besides, I needed to see what was going on, but Maw had her three big knives stuck in the sides of the door frame and she had already done her under the bed inspection twice, so I was stuck. I covered my head and tried to go to sleep, but I couldn't, the laughter haunted me.

"What's the matter with you?" Maw elbowed me in the darkness. "If you don't stop that fussin' you can sleep on the floor, by God."

"Why won't Tady go to bed and leave dad alone." I whispered.

"It ain't her nature; she's like an old dog in heat, besides, he's contributing' to it same as she is. If you ask me, Ruth oughta throw the both of em' out." She pumped her fist into her pillow. "Now go to sleep, and give me some peace."

I was upset, and Maw was gnashing her gums. She knew Tady like a book.

"I know her like a book, and it ain't the bible either." She told me.

"When is she leaving?" Jerry asked the next morning when he found out dad was going to be late for work after staying up with Tady drinking beer until midnight.

"The sooner the better is what I say." Maw said, slamming the refrigerator door shut. "There's no call for her to act that way, she's not changed a bit."

The next morning Tady came into the kitchen wearing a silk nightie covered with a thin red robe that trailed after her like a flame and licked at her fat ankles. She sat down at the table and lit a cigarette.

Dad pounded down the steps and out the front door without his coffee or his lunch and Tady craned her neck to watch him go.

"Now, there goes one good looking hunk of a man." she said.

Mother came downstairs, her eyes looking red and puffy and started sweeping the kitchen floor with great intention. Maw poured her a cup a coffee from the big 40 cup rancher's pot and took the broom out of her hand.

"That can wait, Ethyl's coming over this morning, have your coffee." Maw said.

"Yeah, sit down little sister. Like I told Clydie last night when we were knocking back a few beers, my husband is glad to have a vacation from me, cause I wear him out *every* night." Tady laughed and showed her gold fillings. I saw fire flash across mother's eyes like heat lightning.

Near the end of the week dad was totally hooked on flattery. He was pouring on the *Old Spice* cologne until we had to open all the windows in the house. Pernoon said they could smell him all the way down to Broad Street. But, when he decided to stay home from work on Saturday when he had a chance for overtime, I thought he had lost his mind, he never did that before.

"I think I'll stay home today," he told mother, as he stood in front of the mirror combing his hair and patting more aftershave on his face.

"Why, don't we need the money? You never stayed home from work in your life!"

"Well maybe I want to, that's all. Maybe I'm damn tired of working."

"You better be damn tired of eating too!" She picked up her hair brush and drew it through her long chestnut hair.

"Maybe I'll go back to work, *then* you can stay home and watch the kids. Besides, Jack Rathbone told me just the other day that he missed me at the shoe factory. He said, "Ruthie honey, you can come back any time your little heart desires."

She gave dad a defiant look in the mirror, "So you stay home, and I'll just call Jack."

He slammed out the door and went to work. He was jealous of her, and she knew it.

She still had her figure after four babies, and with her long dark hair and slight overbite, which always gave the impression she was pouting, men went for her like bees to honey. She knew it too, and so did he. That was the cause of 50 % of the fights at the Monkey's Nest and Mom Dago's.

When Tady finally stepped out of my bedroom, she was dressed to meet the Queen. She wore a white suit with a huge yellow sunflower riding on the lapel that bounced when she walked, in tune with her round hips. Matching white gloves, shoes, and a saucy little hat with a white veil completed her "meet the Queen" ensemble.

She came downstairs craning her neck, her heavy perfume hanging in the air like a San Francisco fog. Mother cracked eggs and poured the coffee while she watched Tady through slanted eyes.

"Where's Clydie?" Tady asked casually, as she buttered her toast.

"Clydie, went to work. He has a family to support, you know." Mother told her.

"But I thought..." Tady shrugged her shoulders and smiled. "Maybe tomorrow." she said, biting into her toast and watching mother.

I knew something had to give; the air was thick as oatmeal.

Tady sat tapping her foot nervously, "Oh damn it anyway, I'm all dressed up with no place to go in this one horse town." She gathered her purse and gloves and walked out the front door without saying a word to anyone.

It was later in the day when Valice called. "A word in your ear, Ruthie," she said in her oily voice. "Tady's been here all day at the bar, drinking imported beer."

"What's wrong with that?"

"All day long she's been ranting and raving about you."

"About me? But why?"

She's saying how you act so high and mighty and that someone needs to bring you down a peg, and how she is just the woman to do it."

Valice sighed, "You know what a hellcat she can be and she's full of fire and brimstone.. I just thought I should warn you, she's on her way back to your house right now.

"Warn me? What for?"

"She said when she gets to your house; she's going to teach you a lesson."

Mother laughed and rubbed her chin, "Well she can try if she wants to."

"I mean it, watch your step honey, I've seen her in action and she's pretty tough."

Just then the back door banged open. Tady strutted in and posed by the door, her lower lip jutted forward and her eyes narrowed.

She threw her purse on the table and took off her gloves. Maw ran over and got the big pot, the coffee had been brewing since breakfast and it was lethal. She poured Tady a cup and pushed it towards her.

"Here, have some coffee, we was about to fix dinner." Maw glanced at mother and pursed her lips. She didn't want any trouble and she knew how nasty Tady could be.

"I don't want coffee." Tady pointed at mother, "I want to whip her ass."

"Taddy, they hadn't ought to be a call for that. Ruth never done you any harm." Maw said.

"You can just keep out of it old lady, or you'll be sorry too." She put her hands on her broad hips and walked across the room. "When *I* get mad and walk down the street in Redwood City, people leave their porches and go in the house, and my husband Arthur runs and locks himself in the garage, because nobody messes with me." I decided if she hit my mother, I was going to bite her.

"Tady," mother sighed," I really don't want to fight with you.

"You've had a few drinks and I don't want to upset mommy, but I'm not afraid of you, either." Tady batted a cup off the table and it crashed to the floor. I started crying and went over to stand by Maw.

"You damn well better be afraid of me. Not only can I whip you, but I could have your husband any night of the week if I wanted him," she pointed her finger at Mother, "and you know he'd rather sit downstairs with me, than to go up to bed with you."

"I don't care." mother shrugged, "if that's what he wants to do, let him do it. I don't have my finger up his ass."

To my bug eyed horror Tady crossed the room, pulled her right arm all the way back, doubled up her fist and took a swing at mother, who had the good sense to duck, but before Tady could swing again, mother delivered a solid Joe Louis punch, square on her jaw.

The screen door split open and she landed on the porch, where she lay sprawled out with her garters showing. I thought she was dead until I heard her whimper, like the cries of kittens for their mother's milk.

She was trying to roll over, looking like a big sea turtle on its back. While she was working on this maneuver mother tore upstairs taking two steps at a time, and like a mad woman, she began throwing all of Tadie's lovely clothes and suitcases down the steps and lugged them to the front porch.

She called a taxi to come immediately, and with forefinger pointing to the door she ordered Tadie out of the house.

The last time I saw Tady she was climbing into a yellow taxi with a bloody nose and a stunned look on her face.

The sunflower was gone from her shoulder, and even though Jerry and I looked and looked for it, we never did find it, Earl said if he found the sonofabitch, he was going to bury it.

When dad came home that night and all of us sat down to dinner he asked where Taddy was. Maw and mother exchanged meaningful glances.

"She had to leave," mother coughed, "something came up."

Cousins

My aunt Peroon had three good looking sons by three different husbands and she was single again.

Bernard at 23 was the oldest, and he was like a father to me. When I was 4, he took me shopping for Easter clothes and bought a crate of baby chicks which he let me pass out in every bar on Broad Street. By the time we got home that afternoon, I only had one chick left.

Carl Frederick was the second son, he worked for the city as a ditch digger and he hated it. "I want a career, I want to go places," he said. At 18 he joined the army so he could see the world and learn a trade, (that's what the recruiter told him.) They sent him to Germany where he learned to dig ditches. When he returned home he brought back a ton of little paperback books with naked women in them. He carefully hid them under his mattress in our back bedroom where he was staying with his brother Harold.

Of course Jerry promptly found them and brought them to share with me. When he fanned the pages it made a little movie where the girl's butt moved back and forth and her legs kicked up and down. It was utterly fascinating.

Harold, Pernoon's youngest son was a good looking boy of 15, with light brown hair streaked with blonde and hazel eyes. When he was 5, polio left him with his right foot twisted. Harold refused to wear braces or use crutches. He taught himself to walk with a little hop and a limp, but I never thought of him as being crippled.

Since mother always had a nickname for everyone, she decided to call him "Buddy."

Buddy had a talent for drawing and painting, and he was very good, especially when he drew the Varga Girls, or the nude Calendar girls. They were the creation of Alberto Varga who worked for Esquire Magazine.

I loved to hang over his shoulder when he was drawing them.

"Hey Face," he snapped his fingers at me, "hand me that tube of brown."

I rummaged through the half squeezed tubes of color on his work bench and found one that had brown paint smeared on the outside and handed it to him.

"What do you use the brown for, Buddy?" I could think of nothing on the drawing that would require brown.

"The naked lady. I'm mixing the brown and white to make nude." He began to sketch a profile I moved in and stood at his elbow as he drew the long lashes and perky nose, then the pouting mouth and long Audrey Hepburn neck, followed by pointed breasts and then the legs, long, long legs, and black strap heels, three inches high on her tiny arched feet. The hair was drawn in short swirls and hung in waves down her back and over her shoulders. She sat on a little stool with her chin resting over her shoulder, butterfly wing eyelashes dusting her cheeks.

"She's beautiful, Buddy," I sighed. "I want to look just like her when I grow up." He filled his drawing in with the nude color.

"Fat chance, Face," he chuckled. So it stood to reason that in the second grade when the teacher asked us to "draw something we liked," I drew a naked woman. My teacher, a staunch Southern Baptist snatched me from my seat and sent me to the office in tears.

The vice principal gawked at the perfect breasts on my nude drawing while absently calling me "a naughty child." She called mother to come to the office.

"Mrs. Harris, I want you to look at what your daughter drew in her class this morning. Personally, I find it quite disgusting." She handed mother the drawing and I held my breath.

"She drew this?" Mother held it up to the light.

"Yes, she most certainly did!" The loose skin on Mrs. William's neck trembled and her small bird eyes glittered with indignation.

She had not had the horror of meeting Jerry yet, but he was responsible for her retirement two years later. I heard she tried to hang herself from the jungle gym in the school yard.

"You did real well, honey." Mother nodded to me; she was an artist in her own right. "Except for the legs, they look a little too long, like sausages," she laughed, "you'll have to work on that, but everything else is pretty near perfect."

"You mean to say, you are condoning this,.. this piece of trash?" Mrs. Williams raged.

"She's an artist, just like her cousin, Buddy. Besides, they've got naked people all over the stain glass windows in the churches downtown, so it can't be too awful. Far as that goes, none of us was born with any clothes on," mother folded her arms and winked, "now was we?"

I was sent home. On the way, mother told me sternly that I had better stick to drawing houses and people with clothes on, at least while I was in school and in the company of ignorance.

Aunt Zeta's daughter Joan was four years older than me. When I was 5, Zeta would come over on Friday and take me to her house in Valley View to spend the night. Everything in her house was polished amber wood, thick pastel throw rugs, glass cabinets filled with the Little Golden Books, dolls from Germany that wore everything from bras to fancy lace trimmed panties and silk parasols that opened.

Joan's room was all pink satin wallpaper with girls dancing on their toes, a big maple dresser with a round mirror and lace curtains at the windows. And it all smelled like cinnamon candy and lemon cake icing.

I figured she was lucky; she didn't have to go to Mattie's once a year to get her hair chopped and fried. She had long golden braids to her waist like a princess, each wrapped with a different colored silk ribbon every day that she chose from a silver box. How I wanted those ribbons! My hair was short and fuzzy and plain brown. I didn't look like a princess, I looked like Raggedy Ann.

Over the summer I tanned a dark brown, and when I was eight years old Bernard's wife Betty, pierced my ears. When I went back to school in the fall the kids began calling me Pocahontas and said that my father was Tonto. At recess they chanted, "One little, two little, three little Indians" Maw found me crying on the back porch one night and tried to console me.

"Everybody at school thinks I'm an Indian because my ears are pierced." I cried.

"What do you mean; everybody *thinks* you're an Indian?" She pointed to the front yard where dad was working on the Plymouth.

"Look at your father, he looks just like Tonto, and you favor his side of the family. You have a touch of the South from my side, but you got more war paint than hoop skirts, I'd say." She shook her finger in my face,

"You had best learn to live with it, or wallow in misery for the rest of your life." I wallowed in misery.

Joan had a remarkable gift for instruction and I will be forever grateful to her for teaching me to read when I was 5 years old. She used the "no gain, or you'll get pain," method. If I missed a word she pinched me, not hard, but it worked like a charm. After the first 20 pinches, I could read the Wall Street Journal. My first grade teacher was astounded.

My cousin Eva Jo, (she dropped the "Jo" as soon as she was able to talk,) was Ethyl's daughter and we were like two peas in a pod. She had my brown hair, except hers was shot with amber and gold highlights; hanging around her shoulders in soft waves, and her skin was alabaster. She had lovely hazel hooded eyes like the Madonna in the stained glass window at the Holy Family church on Broad Street. Eva laughed when I told her that, and said the only thing holy about her, was her underwear.

We were both moon babies, I was born late in June and she, early in July, and since we were the same size, we traded clothes. Nearly every weekend Eva stayed with me when I wasn't at Joan's house, because she hated being alone.

Her parents liked to socialize in the bars on Broad Street, but unlike me, Eva hated that scene. They lived on the West side in a small duplex, and they were middle poor, like us.

The Easter we were both 9 years old, dad carefully counted out the money for me on the kitchen table for the light and gas bill and three dollars for the Kay's Jewelry Store payment.

There was extra money for bus fare and a Coke at Kresges on High Street, plus he gave me enough for a new Easter dress and a pair of shoes. Every Easter he thought I should have a new outfit because I had to give a recital on Sunday morning and besides, his Uncle John Thompson was the deacon and his mother's sister Nettie, or aunt Net as I called her, was head of all church related activity at the Valley View Church of Christ in Christian Union.

Uncle John came to our house in his Ford every Sunday morning at 7:45, tooting his tinny horn over and over, over and over until I ran out the door half dressed, my hair stinking like Saturday night's beer and cigarette smoke.

I nodded in church trying to keep awake during the boring monotone of the visiting preachers and nearly peed when I was suddenly jarred awake by his shouts of "Hell fire and brimstone."

Uncle John and his sister Nettie were both determined to save me from hell, and I know for a fact that I was the only child in church that got saved every single Sunday. Aunt Net dragged me from my seat in the last pew, to the front of the church where she forced me to kneel, with her cold bony hands pressed against the back of my neck; my face buried in the yellow mums at the altar. While the choir sang "Rock of Ages," her thin voice rose into the church rafters:

"PPPRAAISE JEEESUS, SAVE THIS CHILD FROM THE EVILLL IN HER LIFE" and the church choir in the front row all nodded their heads in unison and chanted loudly, "AAAAHHH... MAAANNN." So the Easter dress wasn't my idea, it was salve for my Father's pride.

I knew my way downtown, I had been riding the bus, with Maw since I was 3,. I could transfer from one bus to the next, all the way to Cleveland, Ohio if I had to. I had talked Eva into going to church with me on Easter morning and it was no easy feat. She hated all the phony pomp and circumstance, and the row of old bitties that whispered every time I walked past them to hand out the morning programs. They were smug in their assurance that I was the devil's child because I spent Saturday nights at the Monkey's Nest with my parents. Mother said *they* had to be there as well, to have seen *me*.

Eva and I debated whether we should wear a pair of mother's high heels downtown or not. Sometimes we liked to dress like 20 year old women, and mother let us take her purses and wear roses in our hair, and rouge. We decided there was too much running to do, so we wore our Mary Janes.

We had fun trying on all the expensive hats in the French Room at Lazarus department store until we were coldly asked which $95.00 hat were we *really* interested in purchasing. We finally found the dress we both loved at the Boston Store. It had a navy blue taffeta full skirt and red and white striped top with a wide matching belt.

However, Eva had failed to mention that she didn't have enough money; well actually, she didn't have *any* money. I knew I couldn't wear a new dress if she didn't have one too, I knew dad would understand, so I spent the bill money. There wasn't a dime left and we had to walk home all the way from downtown, but it was fun and we laughed about how we would curl our hair and wear tangerine lipstick the next morning. It was fun until I had to tell *mother*.

"Now. . . . let me get this straight," she turned her head to one side like she was deaf, "you did *what*?"

"I spent the bill money." I whispered, fear starting in my feet, and coming up my legs like hot water rising.

"The bill money? You *spent* it?" My chest expanded and the air entered my heart and flooded all the chambers, roaring in my ears.

"You had better answer me, girl!" She stood up, taller than I remembered. I pressed my head against my right shoulder and squeezed my eyes shut. I couldn't speak past the lump in my throat.

"Why are you yelling at her like that?" Dad came in from the yard, his eyebrows knitted together. He was wiping his hands on a rag; he'd been working on the Plymouth again.

"She spent the bill money." Mother pointed in my direction.

"Spent the bill money?" He threw the rag on the table and stared at me through fierce eyes. He had never looked at me like that in my entire life.

I was drowning but I couldn't break the surface as 100 tears fell all at once. Eva stepped in front of me and cleared her throat.

"Uncle Clyde," her voice wavered, "it was all my fault. We wanted to dress alike in new Easter clothes, but I didn't have any money and I didn't tell Jo until we had picked out our dresses and she felt sorry for me. So she bought me a dress just like hers, so we could be twins when we go to church tomorrow.

She looked at her shoes and sobbed, "I'll take it back right now, and pay those bills for you." She hugged me and our tears mingled, fogging her glasses.

"Oh well dammit, come on," he patted my head stiffly, "don't cry, baby. You did the right thing, I'll work it out. . . after while, don't worry."

He sighed, and looked at mother. She clamped her lips together and shook her head. I didn't mention that we had bought matching jackets as well. Like Maw always said, "Sometimes it's best to let sleeping dogs lie."

The Figure Eight Kiss

Eva had a half sister that was 4 years older than she was. Jeannie at 12 was a fragile beauty, with finely chiseled features, light brown hair and soft dreamy eyes. She had a passion for drama though, and aunt Ethyl said it must have stemmed from her Southern Belle roots. If we were out walking, Jeannie would have one hand on her hip and her nose tilted to the side.

"That girl is going to walk into a bus one of these days," Dad said.

Jeannie spent every Wednesday afternoon at the Avondale Theater, watching the horror films. It was how she developed a talent for what she called, "her professional scream." It was a full undulating one minute assault on the senses of anyone within three blocks of the sound.

Maw said it could shatter glass and change the flight patterns of Canadian bound geese. She told Jeannie never ever to try that shit at our house around her fine china or she'd be sorry. Maybe that's why Jeannie offered to teach me the professional scream, just to aggravate Maw, I think.

"First thing you have to do, is to take a huge, huge, huge amount of air into your lungs," Jeannie told me as we stood under the Central Avenue overpass one afternoon. I sucked in a huge amount of air.

"More," Jeannie said, waving her arms. I drew in some more air and she waved her arms again.

"More, more," she shouted, "You need tons and tons of air, more, much more."

I felt my eyeballs expand against my lids but she held her hand up for me to wait before I let the air out.

"Now take the air to the back of your neck and just pretend I have a big hairy spider in my hand that I'm going to stick down your shirt, like this one." She held her hand out and there was the hairy spider!

The scream came exploding out of my lungs into my mouth like a fired cannon and kept rushing out until I was trembling and gasping for more air.

Men came running out of Dildines Bar across the street like sprayed roaches, craning their necks toward the sky.

"Damn, girl!" Jeannie looked awed, "You outdid me by a long shot, I bet they heard that in Cincinnati." She showed me the spider again and it was the stem from a tomato, but the professional scream was born and it stayed with me all my life.

She was full of theatrical tricks, she showed me how to faint at someone's feet, and how to put on a fake slapping fight which we did on the city bus one day and was thrown off by the driver. But the best was the wonderful figure eight kiss. She taught me through endless sessions until I was perfect at it, and half in love with Jeannie by the time she was finished. She also taught me the proper method of gum snapping, which drove mother crazy.

"If you snap that gum one more time, I'll crack your head like a coconut." she told me.

It wasn't long before I was able to employ my figure eight kiss however, on the love of my life, Dickey Lyons.

His father Carl owned the gas station on the corner down from our house and Dickey at 18, was engaged to Lennie, a tall blonde Swede with big breasts who lived next door to him. Dickey was a twin to Elvis Presley and I was simply wild about him.

Every afternoon while Carl was at the house having lunch and Dickey was tending the station, I went down and posed against the gas pumps like one of Buddy's calendar girls in my little short sun suit and flat chest. It never occurred to me that Lennie was any competition for me.

One night Dickey came to our house and asked dad to take him to the Parsons Avenue junk yard to pick up a used part for a car he was working on.

I asked if I could go too, and at first dad said "no," he was very much aware of my mad crush on Dickey. But I wasn't against begging, and finally he relented and let me go. He wouldn't let me sit in the front between the two of them so I sat in the back seat and leaned forward between dad and Dickey.

Dickey smelled like motor oil, cigarettes, and aftershave, but then every man that came to our house on Saturday night smelled like that, except Dominic, and he smelled like olive oil and garlic. Dad pulled into a gas station and went in to get a pack of Lucky Strikes and ask directions while Dickey and I waited in the car. It was now or never, I thought.

I figured it was now, or I might never get my chance for the man I loved. I grabbed him by his ear and when he turned around I laid my figure eight kiss on his beautiful full lips.

I twisted my head around in a figure eight and closed my eyes, just like in the movies, like Jeannie had shown me. It was a split second and I was in heaven. Until dad came back to the car.

"What the hell is going on?" he asked Dickey, who sat staring out the front window like he was dazed. Dad took me straight home and neither one of them would speak to me.

"She was attached to his face like a damn sucker fish, I had to *pull* her off him." Dad fumed to mother, when we came home

"Who in the hell taught her to do that, anyway?"

"Clyde she's only 8 years old, she doesn't know anything about kissing." Mother said.

"Dickey Lyons is 18, and even *he* was embarrassed." Dad yelled.

That just about traumatized me for my figure eight kiss, but I kept quiet and never told anyone who taught me how to do it. Except for Lennie, and she was strangely persistent in wanting to know the particulars of my method.

She said she was just "curious," but it was my personal opinion that Dickey had liked it after all, he just wanted it from adult lips

Mom Dago

When we didn't go to the Monkey's Nest on Saturday night, we went to Mom Dago's bar and grill. It was closer anyway, 3 miles west of our house on McKinley, across the street from the railroad roundhouse. Mom Dago had jet black hair pulled into a bun the size of an airplane tire, on the back of her head. She always wore a black dress with a white butcher's apron, long black stockings and flat shoes. Silver filigree earrings danced from the tips of her ears.

And in case you are wondering, it was Mom who insisted that everyone address her as Mom Dago. When she spoke in her broken English, her voice was dry and husky like autumn leaves. When she talked she used her hands and arms to punctuate her words, nearly all of which, ended in the letter A.

"You likea da….(hands and arms waving,) da spaghett? Mom Dago, she makea dis special fora you." She liked my father and mother very much, but she did not like it that I was with them in her bar after 11:00 p.m. She was terrified the police would drop in and see me there and take her license. Dad assured her that it was all right.

"Hey Mom, Jo's been going out with me and Ruth since she could walk, you know that, there's never been any trouble." He hugged her and she pushed him away, laughing like a girl.

"You good looka man Clyde, but Mom Dago, she know how you lika ta fight, you and thata Cal, he *bad* boy." She wagged her finger at him.

"Mom, I swear, no fighting. We just want to have a few beers and then we'll leave." Dad swore, and at the time, he meant it. He was a man of his word, but the night was young and the man in the black western shirt and Gibson guitar hadn't arrived yet.

Mom's husband Joe, couldn't speak English, and he stayed back of the bar cleaning and napping in the corner. He looked much older than she was. Mother said she thought it had been an "arranged marriage" between two families in Italy.

They had two children, a girl, Micalenni two years older than I was, and a boy about six years old named Joseph. Mom lived upstairs over the bar and had a small room in the back with a table and chairs and a big gas cooking stove. Pots and cooking utensils hung from a wire rack on the ceiling and one wall was filled with shelves of spices and tea, clay bowls and baskets.

It was nearly midnight and I was bored. Roy Acuff was singing about The Great Speckled Bird, "If I had the wings of an angel, over these prison walls I would fly...." A thick fog of cigarette smoke hung like vaporous spirits mingling and floating in the bar. Dad went across the room to talk to his racing buddies, Dominic and Gavoni, leaving mother and me sitting alone in the back booth.

The table was covered with beer bottles, ash trays, pretzel bowls, peanuts and potato chips, along with my two empty bottles of soda pop. Mother sat in the corner of the booth facing the door while I sat on the edge of the seat leaning against her. She looked lovely in her white dress with little red cherries on it and as she tossed her long auburn hair back from her shoulder I saw that she was wearing the "glow in the dark" rose behind her left ear.

Every man in the room who glanced her way knew she was Clyde Harris's woman and they quickly looked away. Except the man in the black western shirt, with the heart tattoo on his hand. Cocky and sure of himself, he sat down in our booth across from me. He had a guitar slung over his shoulder and I could tell right away that he was a fast talker.

"Hey good looking, my name is Paul, what you got cooking?"

Mother didn't answer, but he persisted.

"How about you and me take a little spin around the dance floor?" She blinked and smiled, I had seen her do that before, she was feeling good after two beers, it didn't take much. She was ready to go home, but Paul thought she was flirting.

"Why don't you just trade places with me, little sissy?" He stood up and took hold of my arm. Dad had warned me many, many, many times about strangers. "*Never* let a stranger touch you. *Never* go near a stranger. They can grab you so fast, and they'll take you away. We'd *never* see you again. Then I'd have to kill them and I'd go the electric chair."

"But hell," his voice would break, "I wouldn't even care anymore…because…my baby would be *dead*." I always cried and promised I would be very, very, careful around any strangers at all times.

I had perfected the professional scream, thanks to Cousin Jeannie, who taught me the technique. I had been known to crack mirrors. Maw said no-one was ever going to make off with me, and keep their hearing. I was filling up to scream now, but mother reached over and pulled me against her." Don't put your hands on my daughter." She patted my arm. "This is my baby."

"All I want honey, is one little dance," he whimpered. "You are about the prettiest little thing I've seen in a long time. Come on, a dance won't hurt you none."

Mother took a deep breath, "Tell you what," she pointed across the room, "see that man sitting over there in the blue shirt with his collar turned up?"

"Yeah, I see him, the one with the black hair?" he said.

"Well," Mother said, "go over and ask him if you can dance with me. See what he says. If he says I can, then I will."

"Honey, we are as good as dancing right now, cause even if he says "no," I can *make* him say "yes.""

Paul strutted over to where Dad sat talking to his buddies and I slid down in my seat.

"Are you going to dance with him?" I pouted, "I don't like him."

"Oh hell, no!" Mother laughed. "Clyde's gonna dance with him.

We watched Paul lean down and say something to dad, then dad frowned and looked over at mother and me. Mother waved at him and shrugged, while Paul kept talking.

Dad scraped his chair back and stood up. Paul doubled his fist and drew his arm back, but he was slow and dad delivered a one two punch that floored him. He scrambled to his feet, swung the guitar, and missed my father's head by a fraction. Dad twisted the guitar out of Paul's lilly white hands and smashed it to pieces on the table, sending beer bottles and glasses flying. Other men stood up and shouted, chairs became air borne and weaker women ran for the door.

Mom Dago shouted a long string of words in Italian, and mother and I huddled in the booth and watched the blood, guts, and beer splatter the walls.

"You go in da backa room with Micalenni," Mom Dago came over and took my hand pulling me out of the booth, "hurry up now, they gonna be trouble."

Two black and white cruisers pulled to a screech out in front just as a chair flew through the front window with a man still in it. Everybody was fighting by then.

The scents in the back room were wonderful, garlic and tomato sauce, hot bread fresh out of the oven, and warm chocolate cookies. Micalenni smiled and pointed to a big blackboard she was drawing stars on. She couldn't speak English and I didn't know Italian but we were able to communicate, and I found that I liked her very much. She showed me how to draw stars and gave me hot chocolate and graham crackers layered with marshmallow.

Later that night after the police had gone and everything was quiet, Mom Dago came and took me to the back door

I didn't want to leave, but dad was waiting with mother in the Plymouth and we went home. He spent all day Sunday cleaning Mom's bar and repairing the window. I would have helped, but I had to go to church.

I am sure there will be those well meaning tongue clackers who will think my parents were irresponsible blockheads, taking an eight year old child into a smoke filled bar with tattooed trouble makers hitting on her mother, and her father slugging it out with the offenders. They won't be the first to voice that opinion.

"I find it appalling that Jo is permitted to go out with you every Saturday night in those awful bars." Mattie told mother one afternoon as we were visiting Tippy Toe.

"Well Mattie, Jo doesn't drink beer." Mother laughed.

"Still, those West Side saloons are corrupt; Herb has told me the kind of people that frequent that area. I should think you would worry about your daughter, Ruth."

"Nobody is ever going to touch my daughter and live to talk about it." Dad told Mattie.

"Besides, she likes to visit with Mom Dago's kids and everybody knows her." He ruffled my hair with his hand and grinned, "We keep a tight leash on you, don't we baby?"

They did watch me, but there were times when I could have been in trouble if not for my guardian angels. Like the nice lady Shirley, that frequented Mom Dago's.

She was in her late 40's, tall and wiry with dyed red hair and dark brooding eyes that made me feel uncomfortable for reasons I did not understand. Sometimes, if I saw her coming in the door, I could escape. Sometimes I couldn't.

"My little angel, give aunt Shirley a big kiss and a hug." I was snapped from my seat and my face buried between her huge breasts where she held me struggling for breath until I saw the tunnel of death and a robed figure beckoning me to the other side. When I was finally released, gasping and pale, huge lips pressed a wet Jack Daniel kiss on my cheek.

She always managed to worm her way over to sit at our table by ordering a round of beer as soon as she came in the door and spotted us. Anywhere my father sat down, there was a crowd of his buddies scraping chairs and tables together until it looked like a national convention.

One night it was nearly closing time and mother was nursing a glass of beer, and feeling pretty good. She was leaning on her elbow at the table trying to hear what her friend Peaches was saying over the din of loud voices and shouts in the bar. Shirley pulled me onto her lap and whispered in my ear with a whiskey breath.

"Sweetie, tell your mother that you want to spend the night with auntie Shirley. I have a little pony you can ride and lots and lots of toys. You'll have fun, go on now and ask her."

"I don't want to." I told her, and tried to squirm off her lap but she held me tight.

"Now be nice!" She said sternly, "You go over there and ask her, right now. I just love little girls and I'll be especially nice to you, you can even sleep in my big bed with me. She let me go and I went over to stand by mother's chair but I was silent. Shirley came and tapped her on the shoulder with one of her long red nails.

"Ruth," Shirley held her hands together like she was praying. "I was telling Jo about my little pony, and she is just begging me to let her stay all night, aren't you honey?" I took hold of mother's arm and felt tears sting my eyelids.

Mother looked at me and when she blinked, my heart sank. She was near her three beer limit, and I watched her tilt the half glass that was left and drink it down.

When she looked at me again her eyes narrowed.

"Did you ask Shirley if you could stay with her?" I was shocked; mother was fine as she looked into my eyes.

"No! I don't want to stay with her!" I bore my head into the hollow of mother's neck and breathed in the fragrance of vanilla and baby powder. She held me and stroked my hair, and then she took a deep breath and turned to Shirley.

"Shirley, why would you tell me that Jo wanted to stay with you, when it was a lie?"

"Well, I thought…." Shirley shrugged her shoulders.

Mother set me aside and stood up. "I know what you thought, you thought I was drunk. You thought you could waltz out of here with my little girl." Mother's nose was inches from Shirley's nose.

"For one thing, I don't get drunk when Jo's with me, and for another thing, she doesn't stay with anybody but *me*."

"Besides, I heard you live in a tiny rat hole apartment. I want to know where you keep that "little pony" you're going to let Jo ride."

With her hand on her hips mother turned to the crowd and wagged her thumb at Shirley. "Sounds like a lot of.. *horse shit* to me."

Everyone roared and Shirley ran for the door, but mother walked over and blocked her exit.

"Just so you know, if I ever see you within a city block of my daughter, I'll rip your black heart out and feed it to my dog." When mother shoved her out the door the entire bar applauded.

If I didn't want to go home with Shirley, I was desperate to go anywhere with Steve. He pulled up in front of Mom's one night on a big shiny black and chrome Harley with a huge seat covered in sheepskin. He was wearing a black leather jacket with a spread eagle painted red and yellow on the back .His dark hair spilled forward over his eyebrows, and his full lips were as shapely as a woman's.

He squinted one eye shut when he removed a cigarette from his mouth, using his third finger and thumb to flick it away

I was in love, again. But so were all the females at Mom's, even mother was batting her eyelashes. So when Steve asked *me* if I wanted to take a ride on his bike I said, "Yes, yes, yes."

Dad knew Steve, he worked at the auto parts store and he had taken him for a ride first, after showing him all the inner workings of the bike's mechanisms. So when I wanted to go, dad couldn't say "no."

It would have been bad manners. Steve lifted me onto the big seat and climbed on in front of me. He arched his back and cranked the bike, kicking it three times before it burst into a throaty roar.

"Honey," he shouted over his shoulder to me, "you hold on to my belt real tight now, don't let go, okay?" He made a circle in the street and we headed out McKinley in the direction of downtown. The wind was taking my breath away and I had to press my face against Steve's back.

He took me out on McKinley Avenue past my house and downtown where the big RKO Grand sign cast a golden light on the street. The white twinkling lights blinked like diamonds, mingled with all the yellow and red lights of the traffic. It was so beautiful, like nothing I had ever seen, I was speechless. Then my glitter bow blew out of my hair.

"I lost my hair bow," I shouted to him, "I borrowed it from mother and she'll be mad."

He stopped the bike in the middle of traffic. While I sat on the wide seat with all the automobiles honking and the drivers cussing him, he ran back down the street and found it.

"Here you go, sweetheart," he winked. "Now hold onto it this time."

When he finally pulled into mom's again, my father was waiting with his arms folded and a worried pissed off look on his face.

"Where did you go?" he asked me tightly when he helped me off the bike.

"She lost her hair bow, and we had to go back and get it." Steve laughed.

"I was ready to come looking for you." Dad told him sharply. "I don't usually let her out of my sight." He rolled his shoulder and I thought for a minute he would punch Steve.

"Hell, I thought you was just taking her down the street, not to New York City." he said gruffly.

Train Yards

Growing up across from the train yards had its advantages. Although if you talked to Maw, it was a big pain in the ass, especially on wash day.

"I never seen it to fail," she pounded her open hand on the table, "every time I get the wash hung out, one of those big iron bastards'll come into the yards smokin' and blowin', and throw soot all over my white sheets."

But I loved to watch the trains come in, especially the majestic mountain hogs with huge wheels as high as our back porch roof. They sat over on the back tracks with steam hissing out of their side vents like giant dragons breathing fire. I liked to watch them pull onto the turntable by the roundhouse where they took them in for repairs.

Down the street about ¼ of a mile was the water tower where they filled the steamers before they went out. It was a tall concrete building with a tiny single window at the top. Jerry called it the "Eye." The big locomotives he named, "Deddie Ditties."

"Jo," he said to me one summer evening while we were looking out the upstairs hall window at the "Eye," in the setting sun. "Would you jump off the top of the Eye for a hundred dollars?"

I would have done it for three dollars, but nobody ever came along to make that offer good. The work engines that pulled the box cars came into the McKinley Avenue yards across the street from our house, but the passenger trains crossed the Central Avenue overpass in back of our house.

There was an alley behind us that connected to River Street, a wide gravel road that ran into Central Avenue. There were three frame houses on River Street, their back porches faced our alley. There was the Litter's, and their five redheaded kids on the corner lot, Mrs. Tyler, Maw's elderly black friend next door to them, and Hump Smith with the prize winning rose garden in back of us. At 84 she could run the 100 yard dash in 1.5 seconds if she caught us in her garden.

On the other side of River Street over by the railroad embankment was mother's mulatto friend, Goldie. She lived in a big weathered two story house with her 12 year old son, Casey. Two small frame houses at the end of the street were used as rental's for the railroad.

It was a treat to watch the passenger cars go by on the Central Avenue tracks, some of them were pulled by sleek diesel engines like the Silver Bullet and the American Flyer. Their beauty and speed could take your breath away when they flew past like silver rockets going to the moon.

Jerry and I climbed the concrete arms on the Central Avenue overpass and as the passenger trains flew past we waved at the people in the dining cars, some holding tea cups in their hands as they looked down at us.

One cold winter day when I was five years old, mother took a bucket and we went up on the back tracks to look for coal to feed the big pot bellied stove in our middle room. I had gone with her once before, but it was scary to see the monstrous locomotives coming in the distance, blowing black smoke, with the steam screaming out of their side vents and the thunder under my feet as they drew closer and closer. Mother was careful to stand off to the side of the tracks, but I thought I could feel the wind trying to suck my winter hat off as the train rushed past us.

Sometimes the engineer slowed down to a lazy chip, chop, chip, chop, and one of the guys in the engine house threw some pieces of coal down for her.

When I was in school I sometimes took a shortcut and walked down the tracks to River Street where I could slide down the embankment and be home in half the time. Of course we were warned to expect severe pain, in the ass region if we were caught, which I never was.

Rail walking, or being able to balance yourself while doing tricks on the rails, like walking on your hands, was considered an art form. Those who stayed on the rails the longest when a train was pounding towards them were heroes, unless of course they stayed too long, then they were dead.

When Earl was 6 years old he was forever threatening to go up on the tracks and kill himself. We knew he wouldn't do it; it was just his way of confirming that we loved him when we screamed, "Oh my God Earl! Please don't do it!" After the first nine times though, nobody paid any attention to him. We'd be having dinner and he'd very nonchalantly announce: "I'm going up on the railroad tracks tomorrow."

"Jerry, will you pass me them peas?" Maw wouldn't even look at Earl. He was relentless though.

"I'm going to do it. I'll wait for that 1:30 train to come by, that big one that pulls all the boxcars.. The really *big* boxcars."

"How are you going do that?" I'd ask him, "You can't even tell time yet."

"I don't have to; I can hear the whistle blow at that crossing down the road." He folded his little arms to make sure he had our attention before he went on.

"And when that train comes down the tracks, I'm just going to let it run right over me."

"Hey Earl," Leroy said, "Do you want to go looking for bottles with me tomorrow, down by the dump?"

"Can I go, Awk?" He'd say, all excited.

"But Earl, how can you go," Mother said sadly, "when you'll be run over by a train?"

The best part of living by the train yards came in the spring. That was when Barnum and Bailey came into the yards with the Circus train. I was forced from sleep as the sun edged over the horizon, to the sound of elephants trumpeting, the shouts of male voices mixed with bells, train whistles and music.

McKinley Avenue had magically been turned into a huge circus town full of strange looking people, wagons and animals.

There were giant men with bulging muscles, beautiful women in velvet costumes, the fat lady with a brown beard and tiny people running around doing somersaults. Clowns walked down the street on stilts and rode in funny purple cars with yellow dots on them.

There were rough looking men in slouch hats holding onto chains snapped around the feet of elephants. Young girls in tight glitter costumes walked in the street, and the terrifying roar of the big cats as they were being unloaded from the train for the drive across town to the ball park, where the big top was going up that afternoon.

All the neighborhood kids begged to help put up the tent so they could get free tickets, and the ones that didn't get selected, sneaked in anyway. The midgets with their big heads and short legs were like ants, running around with buckets, looking for water for the animals. A few of them made the mistake of coming into our yard to use the hose.

Maw was out of the door like a trap spider pouncing onto her prey.

"Out, out, out!" She screamed, swinging her broom.

"A bit of water," dramatized the pesky midgets, "for the poor thirsty animals."

Maw thought the circus was composed of beggars and gypsies. She feared they might steal Jerry and try to sell him, or take the yellowed silverware and chipped china from the oak cabinet in the parlor. I couldn't reason with her thinking, because I knew perfectly well that if they took Jerry, they would bring him back the next day.

"Mommy," let them have some water," Mother pleaded.

"Thieving baby snatching bastards" Maw muttered, as she went in the house and slammed the screen door. The midgets ran for the hose before she could come back again.

Later in the evening, Cousin Eva and I went to sit on the Central Avenue bridge where it sloped down on either side into two big concrete arms.

The circus would come down Mckinley Avenue past our house, turn on Central Avenue and then on to the big ball field over on Mound Street. It took them all day to unload from the trains, assemble, and get ready for the long slow walk to the field.

There was the sound of flutes and drums, the rattle of tambourines and bells while the circus performers in their beautiful costumes waved to the cheering crowds.

Jugglers and animal trainers walked beside the big cats as they rolled along in their cages, and of course the painted clowns and pesky midgets. The twelve Clydesdale horses were magnificent as they walked two abreast down the street, leaving enough horse shit behind them to fertilize Iowa. Elephants linked themselves together like fine embroidery, trunk to tail, ten of them in a long line, stepping and swaying like New Orleans funeral dancers.

That night as the elephant's were passing, Eva and I sat on the Central Avenue overpass watching them, especially the cute guy in the white tights with the cape. We decided he had to be a "flyer," the man on the flying trapeze.

I groaned when I saw Ruby Imes, an older girl from down the street come running up to us through the crowd gasping for breath, she was always more than glad to give me bad news.

"Jo Jo, you're in big trouble...your mother, well.... she's out looking for you." Ruby opened her mouth and sucked in air, "And she's real mad. She said you don't have any business being out here after dark with these circus people all over the place, and she said you know it too." More sucking of air, "And...she's got a really big lilac switch with her."

Eva and I scrambled down from the bridge, scraping our legs in the back and snaked around the crowd of people watching the parade. We waited at the curb for a break in the circus, and then we darted across the street between the jugglers and the midgets and more elephants.

I was terrified of the elephants, and even more so when one of them raised his trunk and trumpeted loudly behind me. I nearly fainted though, when he broke free from the line, and headed straight for me and Eva.

Eva and I looked at each other and screamed, our mouths in a perfect square. We ran, and I could feel the ground thumping under my feet as the elephant charged close behind us. I thought of all the Tarzan movies I had ever seen at the Avondale, and I knew that elephants could mash you like a place mat, or pick you up in their trunks and throw you against the wall.

As it turned out, all he wanted was the apples from Mr. Anderson's tree. We just happened to be headed in the same direction. After that incident, facing mother wasn't nearly as bad.

Old Man Glass

Next door to our house on McKinley Avenue was a tiny house with four rooms and an outhouse in the rear of the lot. It was painted hunter green with black trim, and weeds grew in wild profusion in the yard. For years, strange families moved in and out of the house quickly, and for one summer and a winter it sat empty.

One Spring morning an old man in bib overalls and a ring of white hair around his bald head started unloading cardboard boxes from a mud splattered pickup truck and taking them into the house.

Mother and Maw leaned out of our upstairs window until I thought they might fall screaming to the ground, trying to see who he was and what he was doing. Even Cookie came out of his kitchen camp car where it was parked across the street in the train yards on the side rail. He stood on the back porch of the camper, one hand backwards on his hip and the other shading his eyes, his white apron straining to cover his big belly. Maw hobbled quickly across the street, pumping her elbows for added speed, and I followed her.

My nose caught the aroma of freshly baked bread riding the wind out of Cookie's kitchen. He cooked for the section men that traveled with the railroad and made repairs. The camp car faced McKinley Avenue on a side rail that split from the main track to the train yards, and this was their home base.

Cookie knew everything that went on in Columbus. The crew members that followed the camp cars were a tough bunch of leather necked guys and it was whispered that more than a few were ex-cons. Maw squinted as she looked across the street as our new neighbor shuffled out to his truck for another load of boxes.

"What do you make of the old man, Cookie?"

"His name is Oliver Glass, according to him. He came over here last week wanting to know if I was interested in buying any vegetables from him. Said he has a farm outside Milford Center and wants to stay in town to sell at the Farmers Market on the weekends." Cookie laughed and his belly moved the apron up and down.

"He's a nervous old fart, been in the country too long I think." Jerry came flying out of our front yard on his bike between the tall hedges and skidded to a circular stop in front of the truck. When the dust settled, the farmer stared at Jerry. Jerry stared at the farmer. There was something in the air and I could smell it. It was trouble, because where ever Jerry went, trouble wasn't too far behind.

We weren't home ten minutes until the farmer was knocking on our door. Maw answered it." I need to speak to the woman of this here house." His voice was high pitched and it came out through his nose, ending in a soft whistle.

"Which one, old man?" Maw struck her Spanish dancer pose, with her hands on her hips and her eyes narrowed.

"It don't matter to me. I can tell you, what I come to say, just as well" He pointed his finger toward the house next door." That house," he stopped long enough to spit tobacco across our yard, "over yonder there, is mine for the summer. I seen some kids in your yard today when I was unloading my supplies." He stepped closer to the screen door and wagged his finger at Maw.

112

"I come to tell you that I won't put up with those kids on my property. I can make trouble for you, if I get a mind to." He drew himself up by his bib straps, "So happens, I know the Mayor."

"The Mayor?" Maw hooted, "That old thieving sonofabitch? Brother if I was you, I wouldn't brag about it!" She slammed the door in his face.

It was later that afternoon that mother's sister Ethyl stopped in with her daughter, Eva Jo. Eva went upstairs with me to play dolls. Mother was making coffee while Maw set out the cups and saucers.

Without warning the spring afternoon was shattered by a tremendous crash, followed by a shrill scream that hung in the air like an echo. I thought old Hump Smith had found one of the boys in her rose garden again and shot them, like she was always threatening to do. All of us hammered into the living room, our eyes round as silver dollars.

"What happened?" Everyone asked at once. A few minutes later someone pounded on the front door. It sounded like it was the police looking for Cal but it was the old man next door. His bib straps hung around his hips, and his eyes, the color of mud, were ticking back and forth like he was watching a ping pong game.

"My privy was knocked over and I was in it. I could have been KILLED!"

"For God's sake!" Mother said, "Are you alright?"

"Noooo!" His voice rose, "I ain't all right! And it was your boy what done it to me!"

"You mean Jerry?" Maw stuck her face in the doorway.

"If he be the one with the yella hair and them wicked eyebrows, then he be the one."

"Well did you see him do it?" Mother asked.

"I don't need to see the devil, to know he lives. I could tell the minute I laid my eyes on him this morning that he was gonna be nothin' but *trouble*."

"But Jerry wasn't even here, I sent him to Dolder's for milk." Mother pointed to the front yard. "He's coming back now."

"You know," Maw added her two cents worth, "that toilet wasn't built on the square." It was forever tryin' to tip over when somebody was in it, long before you straddled that hole." Mr. Glass pointed a shaking finger at Jerry when he came into the house.

"He done it, and I'd bet my life on it."

I held my breath, he could be sorry he was making that bet with mother, I could see her eyes flashing and the set of her jaw. She stepped out onto the porch and he backed away.

"You listen here old man, I don't like it one little bit that you come over here and blame my son when you didn't see him do it. Didn't you hear what Maw told you? That toilet wasn't built on the square, it always tips like that."

Mother had a really bad temper, but it took a lot to get her crazy mad. "I don't know," she'd say in a dazed voice, "it must be the Smith strain, everything just turns red."

The week before, she'd chased our cousin Red, (same Red that startled Maw out of her nap,) all the way down to Broad Street, smacking him on the head with a pancake turner like she was beating a drum, and him fighting to get away from her. And Red was a grown man. I was 14 before I saw him again.

I looked over at her now as she stood with her fists folded against her hips. Her right eye blinked like a neon sign and I knew her blood must be starting to boil, she was getting mad. I wasn't the only one who noticed it either.

Everybody in the room took three steps backwards in unison, like in the old west when the gunslinger came into the saloon and all the people ran for the back door.

"You keep your kids and that dog," Glass made circles in the air with his finger as he started down the steps, "out of my yard!" Mother walked stiffly back into the house and we sighed with relief. But to our horror, he came back and peered through the screen door with his eyes screwed tight.

"Like I told the old woman," he said in his high nasal voice, "I know the Mayor. I can make a lot of trouble for you people, and don't you forget it." It took Ethyl and me, and Maw, to hold mother back.

From that moment on it was war. Jerry was always pushing dad to the limits anyway, but now it was an incident every weekend, with Mr. Glass pounding on our door with a complaint, mainly about Jerry, and almost always during dinnertime.

"Here comes old man Glass, slidin' on his ass." Maw said one night as we were having dinner.

Dad didn't wait for him to knock on the door. He grabbed Jerry by the arm while he was in the middle of chewing on an ear of corn and nearly pulled the door off its hinges when he opened it. But the sight of the old man rendered my father speechless.

Glass was wearing filthy long johns. From his head to his bare feet he was completely covered in a yellow cream, like a new born baby before the nurses cleaned it. One side of his hair was plastered straight up and fanned out like a feather.

"*MAINEEZZZE!*" he screamed at the top of his lungs, the cords in his neck expanding. "My entire bed was full of *MAINEEZZZE!*"

Dad let go of Jerry's arm and stepped forward to get a closer look at him. Maw was pounding the table in silent hysterics until a piece of chicken caught in her throat, and she quick shuffled into the kitchen for a drink of water. Mother and I sat with Leroy and Earl like zombies, waiting for Jerry's Saturday night strapping, compliments of old man Glass.

"Itus smeared," his voice wavered, "all the way from the head, to the foot of my bed, under them covers. When I got in bed and laid down I stuck my bare feet into a cold hunk of it. I didn't know what it was, then my ear filled plumb full when my head hit the piller." He stopped and stared into space with his mouth open as if he was seeing the horror of it all over again.

Anybody could see that the old man was in a state of shock and I wondered what we were going to tell the hospital if we had to take him in. It also occurred to me that we didn't have a car. Dad would have to put him on Jerry's handlebars and peddle him over to Mt. Carmel.

"I can't understand what you're saying," Dad said. "I don't know what this *maneeze* is, or how it got to be in your bed."

"It's what you put on your sandrige." His nasal voice rose wildly. "It's *MAINEEZZZE!*"

"I don't know what you're tryin' to tell me, man." Dad was losing his patience fast, what in the hell is a *sandrige?*"

"Clyde, I think he means "sandwich." Mother told him. "And maybe, mayonnaise?"

Dad frowned and I saw him struggling to keep a straight face.

"You're telling me, that you had *mayonnaise* in your bed?"

"I AM!" Glass sounded like Billy Graham. "And I'm tellin' you, that devil you call a son, is the one that put it there. The same devil that painted my winders black so I'd sleep all day, thinkin' it was still night My son Herman, he come runnin in to that house the other day and thought I was dead cause I weren't out of the house for two whole days!"

Dad muttered, "Well dammit to hell," and raked his fingers through his hair. He looked at Mr. Glass and shook his head, and then he looked down at Jerry.

"Now tell me the truth boy," he warned him, "Did you do that?"

Jerry folded his arms; he took a deep breath and held it in. I'd seen him do it before when he was in a tight spot. He was exploring his options.

I knew, because his left eye floated toward his temple when he was deep in thought. It was floating now, but the other eye looked sincerely at dad.

"Clyde," he always called our parents by their first name, like a little insurance salesman. It was unnerving.

"I *swear*, I did *not* do that to him." Dad stared intently at Jerry, and I heard the German cuckoo in the kitchen come out of its little door and tweedle six times. The 5:45 was fifteen minutes late as it blew its whistle at the crossing three miles down the road, and next door Little Annie called out her back door in sweet soprano, for Marthana to come in for supper.

"All right!" Dad said, and shook his head up and down. "All right then, I believe you." After all the conflict between dad and Jerry, and all the strappings every time Mr. Glass came over with a complaint, this time, dad believed him. Or maybe, he was just tired of dealing with it. Maybe secretly, he thought the old man deserved it after all, for constantly whining and disrupting our lives and being such a pain in the ass. We were all bug eyed, especially Mr. Glass.

His face turned purple, well actually it was lavender under the mayonnaise. He swung around and walked stiffly to the edge of the porch with his legs spread wide apart and his arms out like airplane wings. We could hear him talking to himself as he went out the front walk.

"I ain't stayin' here no more. Nooo siree, I ain't livin' next door to the devil an him bein' that yella haired boy with the pointed eyebrows,I...I won't do it, I can't"

Glass was packed up and gone early the next morning before any of us was even out of bed and the little green house with the black trim looked as empty as it had for two summers, except that now the windows panes were painted black. The sun was rising and the birds were singing in the trees. I sighed, peace had returned to McKinley Avenue. Well, as much peace as we could stand to live with anyway

A Thorn in my Side

Two houses west from our house, in a weather beaten two story, lived my tormentor. Millie Pemperton was 2 years older than me and all day long she sat in a big swing, hanging from an oak tree in her front yard. She sat there like a spider waiting for a fly, and I was the fly. One night when the moon was pretending it was the sun, I looked out our upstairs window and there she was, sitting in that swing. It made me shudder; it was like she was part of the tree, the bad part.

She had clear bright steel blue eyes like two hard marbles edged in black, and a mass of jet hair in tight little curls around her face. And she was bigger than me, or I thought she was, when she was holding me by the front of my blouse and I was on my tiptoes.

I had to pass her house to go down Central Avenue to the store or to school. She would leap out of her swing as soon as she saw me coming and block my path, standing with her hands on her hips.

"Where do you think you're going? She would demand. Mostly it was to the store for Maw.

"To the store, for Maw." I could feel the tears starting already.

"Give me the money." She held out her hand and I'd give her the money. If I refused, she slapped me silly. Mother tried talking to Millie's mother but it was useless, she was as scared of Millie as I was. For the entire spring and Summer I was beaten and threatened by Millie. My life wasn't worth living; I was terrified to leave the house.

"I never thought I'd live to raise a coward." Mother told me when I came home crying.

"Why do you let her knock you around like that? Didn't I teach you the famous Joe Louis, one two punch" Dad wagged his finger in my face.

"You better start using it."

They didn't understand, I was too afraid to confront Millie. I even bribed Jerry to go to the store when Maw sent me, offering him my quarter that dad gave me for church every Sunday morning.

"You won't get that quarter until Sunday Jo, and then you'll have to give it to the *Screecher* man!" He was right. I could only pray to God that Maw wouldn't send me to the store. But she always did.

"Go down to Dolder's and get me some of them rolls with the cinnamon in em.' Not the ones with nuts, I can't chew those, they hurt my gums, and get me a pound of regular sugar." Maw gave me a dollar. My mind instantly started racing. If I went out the back gate and across the alley, I could sneak through old Hump Smith's yard and go down River Street to Central.

That would work, but the old woman was crazy as a loon, and she and Maw had just had a toothless scream fest over the back fence a week before, because she thought Earl was in her garden picking her roses.

Besides that, she had a whole nest of huge black spiders with yellow stripes down their legs and backs like little jockeys. They had spread their webs across every inch of her yard. I was terrified of spiders, even the tiny ones, but these were like saucers.

I didn't have a choice. I ran out the back door, across the alley and through the gate into Hump Smith's massive garden. The morning sun reflected from her dirty windows, and made rainbow hues on hundreds of spider webs embroidered throughout her yard.

My heart was thumping in my ears, I took a deep breath, I knew I would have to be careful. The yard was like a mine field and I could only guess which way to run, but it was either Hump's yard and the spiders, or facing Millie again.

I took one step forward and a sticky web attached itself to my midsection like a lace overlay.

The unhappy occupant, a gigantic black and yellow spider, drew his legs in, ready to jump. I screamed my professional scream, and all the petals on the American Beauty rose bush next to me, fell off.

I saw Hump Smith streak past her kitchen window like she was on a roller board.

Meanwhile the startled spider on my dress, leaped onto a purple Iris, taking his web with him. I ran out of the gate and down the alley, smack into Millie.

"Okay, what do you have in your pocket?" she demanded.

"I have to go to the store for Maw." I kept my head down; I couldn't bear to look into her cold blue eyes.

She held her hand out. I hesitated too long and felt the sting of her hand on my face, first one side and then the other. When she pushed me down and pulled my hair, I gave her the money

"Where's my rolls and sugar?" Maw asked me when I walked into the house crying.

"Not that little bitch next door, again." Mother said when she saw me.

My mouth was in a circle as I cried. Hump Smith, the big spiders, Millie, and now mother was mad at me, not to mention Maw! Mother took hold of my arm and pushed me out the door.

"You go and get Mommie's groceries, and don't you dare come back without them."

"I can't," I sobbed, "Millie'll hit me, and she hits hard."

"If you don't stand up to her now, you'll be running all your life from bullies just like her. Now either you whip *her* ass, or I'll whip *yours*. The choice is up to you."

I stood by the front gate for a long time, my sobs dried into heaving sighs that hurt my throat. I finally decided I was more afraid of mother than I was of just about anything in the world, lions and elephants included. And even Millie. It was a very liberating thought.

Millie was in her swing as usual, when I walked into her yard. As soon as she saw me she smiled that wicked smile I had come to hate so well and stopped swinging. Her expression changed from a smile to a look of shock though, as she saw me rushing towards her.

In a fraction of a second all the scenes from the past came into my mind, scenes of Millie pushing me down in the mud demanding my lunch money, Millie slapping me until my ears rang and taking Maw's money, Millie pulling my hair and running away with my Easter basket. All the times I had to face mother and Maw and my father, and try to make them understand how scared and helpless I felt.

I wasn't scared as I pulled her out of the swing by the front of her dress. And I wasn't scared when I slapped her so hard it stung my hand.

"Give me my money back, NOW!" I screamed at the top of my lungs. And with trembling hands she handed me the crumpled dollar bill. I couldn't believe it, she wasn't so tough after all. I felt so good; I slapped her again for good measure.

I never saw her after that. Mother was right, I have encountered a few Millie's in my life, one even had a mustache, and although I don't pull their hair and bite them, wisdom has taught me not to wait until a greater fear forces me to face them.

121

The Bradley Bunch

After Millie's family moved out of the old decaying two story house on McKinley Avenue, a new family moved in. Maw said they were distant cousins from somewhere way back on the German side of her family and I believed her because they were all blonde and sturdily built.

Marcie Bradley and Jorg had four children, all of them with names beginning with the letter D. Dena and Dale were the twins, followed by Dora, Dirk and the baby, Divas.

Marcie was a blonde Lucille Ball, with the same kind of brain cells. I was surprised when she and mother became quick friends, exchanging recipes and borrowing sugar from each other.

The summer they moved in was the hottest one on record, the temperature rose to 100 degrees for three days, and there was no sign of relief. All the green blinds in our house were pulled down to the window sills and fans were set up in the kitchen and dining room. It was little comfort, the air was close and sticky and the dark house was depressing. Tempers flared and mother and Maw were like two dogs fighting over a bone.

"Why are you rolling out that dough?" Mother asked Maw one day.

"I'm about to make biscuits for dinner tonight, if you'd get up the gumption to start them beans boilin."

"You surely aren't thinking of starting up that oven in this heat are you?"

"No, I was gonna stick em' up my ass and bake em' that way." Maw slammed the dough roller down and walked out to the porch. Mother went over to see Marcie and give Maw some time to cool off. She was laughing when she came back a little later.

"What canary did you swallow?" Maw spoke in lemon drops, with her brows drawn.

"When I knocked on Marcie's back door she yelled for me to come on in. For all she knew, I could have been the milkman. Well there she was, standing by the kitchen sink peeling potatoes, and the only thing she had on, was a Kotex. She said it was too damn hot to wear anything else."

"I don't see where that's anything to laugh about," Maw grumped. "What if her children'd seen the likes of that?"

"Marcie took the kids to her mother's house while she went to look for a job this morning. She said their landlord told them the city might condemn that old house. Seems the floors in the upstairs are rotting from the leaking roof. She said they'll need extra money if they have to move, so she wants to go to work if she can find a baby sitter."

"Maybe I'll go over and baby-sit for her, I need the money. I never was one to live off of anybody's scraps of food." Maw tilted her chin up and looked down at mother as she sat at the table.

"Oh mommy," Mother laughed, "you couldn't keep up with those little kids, and they have a baby that's just learning to walk." But Maw took off her apron and hung it on the hook behind the stove and started out the back door to the porch.

"Where are you going?"

"I worked all my life, and by God I can work now. I don't need anybody tellin' me what to do." I watched Maw hobble down the alley on her cane and turn in at the Bradley yard.

"Marcie won't hire her! She's too old; Marcie needs a young girl to keep up with all those kids. Mommy is just doing this to upset me, but I won't be upset!" Mother threw a spoon across the room and went stomping upstairs. Maw came back an hour later, her face beaming.

"I start tomorrow morning, at 6 on the dot!" She held her head back until I could see the black hairs in her nose. "While I was over there talking to Marcie the phone rang and she got herself a job, so she hired me on the spot."

"She said there's not a speck of work for me to do, except see to it that the children has a little lunch. Of course, I said I'd do the morning dishes and make the beds, since she *is* payin' me twelve and half dollars a week."

"Mommy, how do you expect to get up and down those steps over there, when you can hardly do it here? And how will you run after those older kids?" Mother was sitting at the table with both hands on her hips, the cords in her neck standing out as she thrust her head upward.

"I ain't as old and near death, as some people would like to think." Maw shouted.

The first night after her new job Maw came home with mashed potatoes in her eyebrows and hair. She went over to the stove and poured herself a cup of coffee, then sat down and wearily stirred in cream and sugar while we all waited to hear what had happened.

"They was a fightin,' and it was just awful," she shook her head. "I tried to step in, but it wasn't any use."

It was 98 degrees outside, but Maw looked like she had just come in from the frozen tundra with frost on her eyebrows. As she talked, I saw there was mashed potatoes pasted on the little cat whiskers that grew at the corners of her mouth as well.

"Those kids were fighting, mommy?"

"Not the kids! It was Marcie and Jorg. He came home and saw her all dressed up from her new job, and he got real red in the face. One thing led to another and next thing you know he grabbed the bowl of mashed potatoes; you know how I make them all fluffy with the baking powder and the whipped egg?"

"Did you use the Idaho bakers or the little red potatoes, mommy? Remember how those red potatoes went flat last time we tried to whip them?" Mother pointed out.

"But what happened at the Bradley's?" I shouted.

"Well! Jorg grabbed that bowl of potatoes while I was whippin' em' with their electric mixer, and there I stood with potatoes flyin' everywhere."

"That fool dumped the entire bowl on Marcie's head and walked out. And don't you know, she went runnin' after him, with that bowl still on her head? After a bit he came back with his tail dragging and apologized to me like I was the head Nun down at Holy Family. Said he's got a "flash temper and don't mean nothing by it at all."

"I think you should quit right now mommy, and let them find another baby sitter."

Maw pointed her finger at mother, "And I don't need you runnin' my life like I was some feeble minded old woman, either."

Two days later mother was on the phone with Nora when Jerry walked in the back door and tapped her on the shoulder.

"I have something to tell you, Awk."

"In a minute, go get me a drink of water, I'm talking to Nora." He brought her a glass of water and leaned against the wall with his arms folded.

"What do you want to tell her?" I asked him.

"Jo, it's an emergency, and it's only for Awk to hear." He had the insurance man's tone to his voice.

I started to leave and he added, "Besides, it's about Maw."

"What about Maw?" I half turned in my tracks, and he grinned.

"She's *stuck*!" He burst out laughing and covered his mouth with his two fingers, rolling his eyes in the direction of the ceiling.

"Who's stuck?" Mother hung up the phone and went to the stove to make fresh coffee for dinner.

"Maw!" Jerry pointed to the Bradley house. "Maw's stuck in the ceiling."

We rushed over to the house and into the living room. High up in the 12 foot ceiling there were two white stumps sticking out of a hole, with chocolate colored support stockings drooping around the ankles and black lace up shoes moving in the air, peddling an invisible bicycle.

We hurried upstairs to find Maw holding onto the leg of the iron bed with the hook end of her cane and her glasses riding on her upper lip. It took mother and me and the three boys to pull her out. After we made sure her bones were still connected we walked her back home, all of us clustered around her like nuts on a bar of peanut brittle.

Mother made her a warm foot bath and I poured her a hot cup of coffee with extra cream and sugar. She had not said a word since we rescued her from the hole, but now she sighed deeply.

"There's no fool like an old fool," she kept her head down as she stirred the coffee.

"Does that mean you're going to quit?" Mother asked her.

"I expect I better, or else get myself a damn parachute!"

"Maw, you can't quit NOW!" Jerry looked worried.

"Why not?" I asked him, I knew he had a big crush on the younger Bradley girl, but Maw wouldn't let him come over there anyway while she was baby sitting.

"Jo, they're getting a *television set!*"

My hair stood on end, everybody was talking about television and everybody had one, but us.

Maw never went back to her baby sitting job, but Jerry and I, Leroy and Earl, spent the entire summer on the Bradley's front porch with our heads jammed together looking in the window at their new television.

After a while they got sick of us commenting on the programs and Jerry licking at the window screen when Marcie made buttered popcorn.

They pulled the shades down and we couldn't see anything, so we sat on their porch and listened to the shows. In the fall it became cooler and they had to close the windows, but they left the blinds up and we could see the programs, but now we couldn't *hear* anything. We quickly learned to read lips and all of us became experts.

To this day I can tell what someone is saying at a rock concert 20 feet away.

Earl punched a guy in the eye once, when he saw him mouth the words, "That's Earl, he's a real bastard," across a crowded room. We've been called a marvel of modern times.

As Maw would say, "God works in mysterious ways, His wonders to perform." But given the choice I would rather have had the television set.

The Bradley's complained, and eventually dad did manage to buy a Motorola. It was in a mahogany chest as big as a casket, with a viewing screen the size of a man's wallet. We glued ourselves to the set every night, sitting shoulder to shoulder, all of us bent forward in a half circle while the blue screen reflected the programs in our pupils.

The Bradley's bought a bigger television and moved to the hilltop before anyone knew they had gone. The world continued on without us, because if you left the living room, you lost your place forever. By the time I saw the Bradley's again, the oldest boy had grown a mustache and Marcie was a widow.

The Door Stop

Not only did we consider ourselves fortunate because we lived across the street from the train yards but we were only a mile and a half from the city dump. All manner of items could be found on the dump. Jerry once found a female mannequin. He tied a rope around her neck and hung her naked from the McKinley Avenue overpass. It caused a delightful number of fender benders.

You had to be careful walking on the dump because there were areas that had been burning and smoldering since 1901, according to dad. He warned the boys to stay off the dump, it was dangerous and it was germy. Mostly it was germy.

But Earl continued to come home with his shoes still smoking, loaded with treasures which he promptly buried in the back yard, like a dog with a bone. Most of the junk was given to mother first though, for her inspection. One day the boys brought her a beautiful door stop that they had found laying in tall weeds by the back railroad tracks.

It was so heavy, that they had to haul it down McKinley Avenue in Leroy's wagon. It was olive green, flat on the bottom and had a beautiful brass top that came to a perfect point. And, it was made in the USA, which was important to mother, she didn't want anything made in Japan. Not after what they did to Cousin Bernard in the big WW ll.

It was a perfect doorstop, at night you could tip it over with your foot and roll it against the wall, next morning it was rolled out again and placed by the door. Maw loved it.

Dad used it one time to sink tomato stakes when he couldn't find his hammer, but it proved to be too heavy for work of that nature. We used it for just about everything for three years, and mother even thought it might make a nice lamp until one Saturday afternoon

Leroy came running up the back walk in a fit of frenzy, screaming mother's name like a wounded bird.

"Awk! Awk!" His black eyebrows arched into his hairline over wild protruding eyes.

Mother dropped the knife she was using to peel potatoes and ran to the door. "What in the hell is the matter?"

"It's that doorstop Awk, it's the doorstop!"

"The doorstop?" Maw elbowed behind Leroy as he ran through the house to the front door, with me and mother following close behind.

He got down on all fours and thrust his neck forward, examining the metal doorstop from the brass tip to the olive green base. Sweat beaded on his forehead and his Adam's apple quivered. "Awk, you had better get on the telephone and call the United States Army right now." "I'm not going to call anybody until you tell me what's going on." mother said.

"I was at the Avondale," Leroy sighed, showing his teeth, "I went to see that new Tarzan movie, you know, the one where he goes to New York?"

"Yeah," I said, "I heard that was a good one."

"Well I never got to see it, Jo!" He shouted. "There was a newsreel on, and it showed how this factory used to make shell casings for the war."

"What's that got to do with Tarzan?" I asked. I had a thing for Tarzan that little skirt he wore drove me crazy wondering what was under it. I envied Jane, but I thought Cheeta was a real pain the ass.

"Jo, it hasn't got anything to do with Tarzan!" He shrieked. "That newsreel started me to thinking," he wiped his mouth on the back of his hand, "that *this* could be an Army shell."

"So?" I asked.

"So if it's loaded, it could blow up the entire house."

Everyone turned in unison, like Broadway dancers and ran for the kitchen, nearly stampeding over Maw who used her cane to beat us out of her way.

Later that day after mother had called the military to ask about the shell, Maw was cutting noodles on the kitchen table when she called out to mother. "Ruth, I think Carl Frederick just walked past the back porch."

"Mommy, Carl Frederick is overseas, he's in the Army. Didn't you hear Annie say last night that she just got a letter from him in Germany?"

There was a loud knock at the front door and two men in Army uniforms stood on the porch, ramrod stiff like store mannequins, their lips pressed tight. Several more soldiers in fatigues were scouting around outside the house.

"Mrs. Harris?" One of the men handed her an ID card with his name on it.

"Sergeant Phillips, with the Special Services Unit, United States Army." he said sternly. "Someone called about a shell casing that you were concerned about? I assume you were referring to a United States Army rifle casing, of course, and not a shell."

Maw called out from the kitchen where she was still cutting noodles, "What does old man Glass want this time?"

"I was the one that called," Mother turned around and pointed to the doorstop, "because my son wants you to look at *this*. He saw it in a newsreel and thinks it might be active." Mother was standing alone, Sergeant Phillips and the other soldier had leaped off the porch and were standing out by the road. Sergeant Phillips cupped his hands over his mouth and called to mother, speaking in loud slow tones as if she were a robber holding hostages in a bank.

"Evacuate the house! IMMEDIATELY!"

Mother was confused. "Do you want us to bring it out to you?"

"NO! NO! NO!" He waved frantically, "Just evacuate the premises! Immediately!!"

After rolling the doorstop to the corner with her foot and setting it against the wall, (old habits die hard,) she went in the kitchen to turn off the skillets and the coffee. Dinner could not be allowed to burn just because she was told to vacate the house immediately, besides, *immediately* to mother meant when she was good and ready, regardless of the circumstances.

Mother had to drag Maw outside who was bitching about her noodles and raving that the Army was just like the damn Yankees that burned Atlanta.

Two men dressed like space invaders walked spraddle legged into the house in plastic jumpsuits. They wore helmets that came down over their shoulders. They picked up our doorstop with long metal tongs and put it in a steel padded box.

I thought about the boys digging that thing out of the weeds and loading it in the wagon and pulling it down the road as it bumped and rolled for two miles. I thought about dad using it to pound the tomato stakes and Maw knocking it over with her cane at night, to roll it against the wall. I laughed at the caution of these egg headed sissy's, it never blew up because we never thought it would, our fear wasn't there to ignite it, but now I felt certain that it could explode, because they feared it, they gave it the power.

The Army called a few days later to say that the shell wasn't loaded after all. If it had been, they told us, it could have leveled a city block. When Nora heard about it, she fainted.

Mother called the Army back the next day. "Do you think you people could return that military shell you took from my house? The boys found it for me and I'm kind of sentimental about it." she sighed. "Besides, we can't keep the front door open without it."

They brought it back the next day and it's still there.

Are You The Lady of The House?

Mother hated door to door salesmen. She felt they were an invasion of her privacy and she wouldn't talk to them. One day in March I was sitting on the back screened in porch with her. She was sewing and I was drawing my calendar girls when I saw a man boldly lift the latch on the back gate and come up the walk.

I say boldly, because my cousin Buddy's, yellow mongrel, Prince,(with the head of a pit bull and the body of a Chow,) was tied by the fence to a soft rope looped through a ring attached to his collar so he wouldn't choke. Earlier that month he had chased the mailman and buried his shoe somewhere in the neighborhood. The post office was strangely upset and demanded we keep him tied up or Maw would have to go downtown for her Pension Check once a month.

Buddy rescued him when he was a puppy, after he saw him being terribly mistreated. It was through his kindness and the love of the Harris clan that Prince thrived. He loved children and was loyal to those he trusted but he could be terrifying for anyone outside this circle, especially trespassers and *especially* salesmen. He might spare you if you knew the password though, "Good dooog, *gooood dog.*" But

Prince could strike primal fear in both man and beast, and for good reason, because he was first and foremost a protector.

Prince was salivating and lunging forward on his rope while the man continued casually up the walk. I thought this guy must be very brave or very stupid.

It might have been more intimidating if the dog was barking, but Prince couldn't bark, he could only growl like a grizzly bear. Buddy said Prince's former owners might have beat him for barking when he was a puppy and now he'd just plain forgot how to do it.

"Don't say I word, do you hear me?" Mother whispered to me as the guy approached the porch.

I nodded and concentrated on my drawing while he pounded forcefully on the screen door.

"You must be the lady of the house," he shouted over the racket of the sewing machine. Mother kept sewing with her head down and her elbows arched up like wings.

"You must be the lady of the house!" He pulled on the door handle with both hands but it was latched. He waved his arms at her and shouted but she peddled even faster until I thought I saw smoke coming from the old Singer. This continued for several minutes when all at once she abruptly stopped sewing and began singing in a thundering voice "AAAAMMAZING GRACE, HOW SWEEEEET THE SOUND." I stopped drawing and looked at her, I knew she could be crazy on occasions but this was scary even for me.

When I thought things couldn't get any weirder Prince stopped thrashing against the rope. His eyes closed and his big mouth pulled back in a grin. I realized he must be remembering when mother sang to him when he was a puppy. He stretched his neck and howled with her.

"Go to hell, you deaf sonofabitch," the salesman said as he turned to leave. He was fumbling with the gate latch when she came down the walk with her arms folded.

"Yoo hoo, hold on there a minute, will you? You know, I'm not really deaf; I just don't like people invading my privacy. But I have someone right here," she leaned over and untied Prince, "that will be glad to invade *your privates.*"

Giving credit were credit is due, the guy did clear the fence from a standing position. I believe he made it to the end of the alley. That was when I heard a dull thud followed by a piercing scream. A few minutes later Prince trotted back through the gate and dug a hole in the yard. It was a nice deep hole and he dropped the handle from the sample bag in, along with one very nice, leather Italian shoe. Mother said it was a pity we didn't know any one legged men. She petted Prince between his ears and gave him a cookie.

"Good dooog," she said. "*Goood dog.*"

I did feel sorry for the kid that came to the house selling the KIRBY sweeper though. He was young and enthusiastic. Ethyl and mother were in the middle of spring cleaning when he innocently knocked on the door.

"So, I see you two ladies are cleaning. Good, I have just the item you need." He presented the KIRBY and all the attachments to clean the rugs, blinds, drapes, even deodorize the mattress.

"Honeypie, she's not interested." Ethyl told him, but mother surprised her and opened the door to let him in. He was all smiles while he demonstrated the wonders of the new sweeper.

He took months of dust out of the drapes, sucked the old oriental rug until it began to show the red and gold colors of its youth, ran a brush coupling along all the baseboards, vacuumed the sagging sofa, adding the deodorizer powder. With each finished task mother said, "Show me more."

He went upstairs to vacuum and deodorize all the mattresses, watching nervously while Jerry and Earl went through his bag of attachments.

"Hey now, what did he do with that piece of tubing?" He asked Jerry after Earl left.

"Oh you mean, Earl?" Jerry asked.

"Yes, I need that tubing, it goes on the sweeper."

"He's probably already buried that. You can go ahead and ask him where it is, but he might get mad and bite you."

Jerry's head started shaking violently from side to side and his tongue slid over his lower lip, stained purple from grape popsicles. "We allll biiite." he said, in a strangled voice.

The kid was still cleaning when dad came home from work. Sweat streaked his face and he had long since shed his jacket and tie. It was 5:00 when he put the sweeper attachments in his bag, (except for the ones Earl buried,) and handed mother a long sheet of paper.

"What's this?" she said.

"A contract for the sweeper," he sighed, "you'll need to sign it."

"I'm not buying that sweeper, it costs too much."

"But I cleaned your entire house," he sobbed, "why didn't you tell me sooner?"

"I didn't want to interrupt. You looked like you was having a good time, you never quit smiling all day. Besides, you came here on your own accord, I didn't call you, did I?"

"You mean I wasted all day here for nothing?"

"But it wasn't for nothing! Look at how clean everything is and how nice it smells. I couldn't have done it without you. Come on, stay for dinner. We're having leftovers."

Dad felt so sorry for the kid that he bought the sweeper and Earl had to spend the summer searching in the yard for the attachments he had buried.

Acid Holes

Every year on the Saturday before Christmas, Columbus Metal Products gave a big party for its employees and their families. They held it in the cafeteria and there was a Santa Claus which I recognized immediately as Mr. Donley, the president of the company. There was ham, turkey, six kinds of cheese, baked beans, cake and tons of ice cream with little Santa's on them. Dad took us on a tour of the shop and showed us the big boiling vats of acid that he worked with to electroplate the parts that came through the plant. It had a stinging odor that hurt my nostrils and I could see why it put holes in his shirts and pants.

The past summer for my birthday he had made me a wide chrome bracelet that he formed around a coke bottle and plated it. He took it to a jeweler and had "Valice" engraved on it. I loved that bracelet, but I let a boy in my class wear it one day, and he never gave it back. His mother said he lost it, and that was that. It was another Green Bike incident in my life.

There were speeches from the management about how well the shop was doing, thanks to the wonderful hard work of all its employees. Mother called it the "ass kissing" speech. Even though my father was putting in long hours now, he was still bringing home a meager paycheck, barely enough to keep his family fed.

Any suggestion of a raise was always out of the question. Because the shop did not have a union, the men were powerless to do anything about the working conditions, which were horrible.

When the union was suddenly voted into Columbus Metal, everyone in the executive office was stunned. They were all positive it was one of the loud mouths in the shop. No-one ever suspected it was the soft spoken man with the acid holes in his clothes, with a lot of help from his feisty wife.

Mother decided after the first three years that she couldn't stand the simpering women from the shop that were in charge of the company Christmas party. So she opted to stay home. All of us kids went though, but we were gravely warned.

"Eat only one serving, and always use your napkin. Don't leave the cafeteria for any reason and never ask for seconds. And you had better remember to say,"Thank you, and excuse me, too." She warned us.

Jerry had three servings, refused to use his napkin, and got lost in the factory. After the party, we were driven home by the "simpering women." Dad and Earl rode in the car in front of us, with me, Jerry and Leroy following behind with the women and the leftovers from the party.

"We've wrapped up all the lunch meat and left overs from the party for you and your hungry brothers." The blonde lady in the red suit sitting next to Jerry told me, and then she leaned over to talk to the fat woman in the front seat as if I couldn't hear what she was saying.

"There are four of them, and can you believe it, another one is on the way? They must be absolutely starving with all those mouths to feed." She was talking about my family. She wagged her finger in my face.

"You be sure and tell your mother not to let the children gobble all this food up at once, or they'll get sick, especially the ice cream." I told mother as soon as I got home, word for word, while she stood with her arms tightly folded across her chest and her foot tapping on the kitchen floor. Maw said I was a blow gut, because I told everything I heard.

Mother threw all the food out. Dad was in a rage.

"Why in the hell did you do *that*?"

"It was spoiled," she told him.

It was the last year we went to the Christmas party.

The summer that I was nine years old the shop had a big picnic, in one of the State parks, and mother consented to attend. Once she set the executives wives straight, by telling them we didn't need their food, nor did we want it, and then she was able sit back and enjoy herself.

They had arranged an array of games for the children to play but the adults were enjoying the targets set up for archery. Mr. Donley, the boss, owned a beautiful bow that he'd had made in California, it was light weight and had colorful carvings down the front. I desperately wanted to use that bow, and I knew how.

My cousin Buddy was an expert archer, perhaps it was his artist's eye for detail but he could hit any target he aimed for and he had taught me how to do it as well.

I had watched him when he pulled back the string on the bow and after a second of silence I heard the twang of the string and saw the arrow hit the bulls eye. After much whining and begging on my part, he let me try it, and even though it bruised my left wrist purple halfway up my arm, I got pretty good at hitting what I aimed for.

Dad and I sat on a bench in the park drinking cokes and watched the ass kissers in the shop miss the target time and time again, hoping to impress Mr. Donley, and failing. Finally he asked dad if he wanted to use the bow and try his luck.

"I might look like an Indian, but I don't know anything about bows and arrows," he laughed. "But my daughter Jo, now she knows something about that, don't you baby?"

I pressed my head against his shoulder and tucked my lower lip up under my teeth. I was painfully shy around strangers, especially if they were authority figures.

"Come on honey; let's see if you can do any better than these guys." Mr. Donley pulled me over to where everyone was standing and handed me his bow. It felt like the same weight as Buddy's bow.

"Jo, this is probably too heavy for you. Let me see if I can find my wife's bow, it's a lot lighter," he said.

"This is fine," I said, "I can use it." He looked dubious but he handed me an arrow and I heard one of the guys snicker. "Hope she don't go aiming that arrow at the kids."

The target was a red bull's eye across the field, leaning against a pile of hay. Buddy had told me the first time I tried his bow, "You gotta take a deep breath," he said, "hold it in and then let it out real slow, to steady your hand."

I took my stance, drew the bow back and took a deep breath.

"Eyeball your target," Buddy had told me, "and set it in your mind, *see* it, and *see* your arrow striking it. Imagine it going down a tube right into the target."

I looked intensely at the target then closed my eyes, I could still see it. I opened my eyes and aimed, letting the arrow fly. When it struck the center of the eye dad yelped like a puppy.

For the rest of the day Mr.Donley and I took turns at the bull's eye. The brown nosers stood to one side with their arms folded, grumbling amongst themselves and my father couldn't stop smiling

"I sure was proud of you today, Snake." He cuffed me against the side of my head. "You really showed em'." I went to see Buddy as soon we got home, I couldn't wait to tell him how I had aced the target, and showed up the brown nosers in front of Mr. Donley and how proud dad had been of me. He listened carefully and then rubbed his chin in deep thought.

"Well that was just great, Face!" He winked, "but what if you'd *missed*?"

The Privy

Once, a long time ago we had a nice bathroom off the kitchen but dad ripped all that out, something to do with a faulty leach bed, and he built an outdoor privy in the back yard. It was no ordinary privy either; the hole under it was as deep as the Grand Canyon. You could go in the privy and pee, walk to the house and up the steps, before you heard it splash in the bottom of the hole.

Dad and Cousin Bernard dug the hole. They dug it until I couldn't see the tops of their heads anymore and Buddy ran out of rope to send the bucket down for dirt from the dig. He kept adding and adding to that rope.

"Hell Face, it looks like they're going to dig this thing to China," he told me.

The walls in the hole were carefully laid with concrete blocks and mortar. Bernard drove truck for a concrete company on McKinley, so he was able to get a big discount for dad on the blocks.

The privy itself was all concrete blocks with a nice pitched roof and a heavy wooden door. There was a long wooden seat with three big holes and two baby holes on each side, facing each other. I wondered how anyone could find three adults and two children who all had to pee at the same time.

Maw kept a chamber in her room, a small china pot with a lid on it that she emptied every morning. There was another pot in my room, it was white metal, with a lid as well, and on cold winter nights when the temperature dropped to zero and all of us kids used it, it was brimming by morning.

The tightrope walkers in the circus had nothing on mother and Maw, trying to carry the full pot down the steps and out to the privy without dropping its foul contents.

When Mother's fifth child David, was two years old, I was walking with aunt Pernoon one night. Mother and her sister Ethyl were walking ahead of us on Central Avenue. We had gone to Dildines, a bar down the street from us by the viaduct, to get two one gallon pickle jars filled with draft beer.

"Mother shouldn't drink any more beer," I told Pernoon, "she's getting fat."

"Your mother's not fat, baby doll, she's going tohave another kid, she's knocked up again." Mother was sick all the time with the baby and it was too much for Maw to carry both of the pots down the steps. So from then on, except for her and Maw, everyone had to go outside at night to pee, no matter how late or how cold it might be.

It was horrible. I would drink a big bottle of RC Cola and nestle into the warm bed under the crisp sheet, the army blanket, and the 10 pound quilt, and drift off into a warm blissful sleep.

About three hours later, wide eyed and full of regenerated RC Cola, I had to pull the covers back and step out onto the cold linoleum. Walking on my toes until I could find my coat and shoes, I ran down the steps and outside to the cold dark privy.

Peeing in the yard was not allowed. The steam rising up from that hot liquid in the zero degree weather was like smoke from the steel factories in Philadelphia.

"Did you pee in the yard last night?" Mother would ask me.

"Yes," I'd confess and hang my head.

"I thought so, there were yellow spots in the snow don't do it again."

Summer was just as bad. You could run outside in your underwear, but the toilet was dark and scary. And the spiders were enormous creatures with hairy legs and weird configurations on their backs, but these were different from Hump Smith's, these were neon. I was certain they hid under the seat, just waiting to bite me on the butt with their poisonous venom. As if that weren't enough, I always imagined some creature like Swamp Thing, clawing his way up the big hole to drag me down into that muck. It took Buddy's wisdom to snap me out of it.

"Come on Face, what kind of a creature would want to live in *shit*?" It certainly was food for thought.

Jerry was scared too, but he had a solution. He built enormous fires out of the Spiegel catalog. One of his fires scorched the ceiling of the privy.

"Are you playing with matches in that toilet, boy?" Dad asked him one day.

"No." Jerry answered.

"Are you lying to me?"

"No Clyde. I am not lying." Jerry insisted, fingering the matches in his pocket

One evening in April mother went to the hospital, and late the following night Dad came home smiling.

"It's a beautiful little girl, we named her Marilyn Rose."

I jumped up and down I was so happy, a girl at last, after four boys. It had been a long hard labor, a breech birth and the baby wasn't well, she was thin and her skin was still red when she came home from the hospital a week later. All the babies that mother birthed were fat and peach colored, even her first son Lester, and he was still born. She talked about him all the time.

"I should've listened to Clyde and gone to the hospital, but I wanted to have the baby here at home. I had an old man in his 80's for a doctor, and the baby was so big I was scared. I had a terribly long labor and they thought I was going to die, my lips and the tips of my fingers turned blue."

"The baby weighed 14 pounds when he was born and his hair was coal black like Clyde's, and curled tight against his head. I held him and he was so beautiful, he looked like he was three months old, just sleeping in my arms, but he was dead." Tears sprang to her eyes every time she told me the story, and every time, I cried along with her.

Mother and Maw fattened Marilyn up, they went to Amlin and got fresh milk from the Amish and fortified it with maple syrup. She grew into a beautiful little girl with butter curls and blue eyes.

Except for David, the boys gave her a hard time, but she quickly learned how to stand her ground and by the time she was three she could hold her own with the best of them. It wasn't surprising then, when sewer lines were finally installed on McKinley Avenue and dad put the new bathroom upstairs, that Marilyn should declare herself the first one to pee in the new toilet.

It was weeks before I could remember that we had indoor plumbing. I would get out of bed, trudge downstairs, yawning and scratching all the way. I'd have my hand on the door of the privy before a big smile crossed my face and I remembered, my God! I could pee in the *house.*

Prisoner's Quarry

In back of our house on Central Avenue, the viaduct sat like a gray stone Mayan God. The railroad tracks going over it passes by Prisoners Quarry two miles west of our house. During the twenties the quarry was a limestone pit where the prisoners from the Ohio State Penitentiary chiseled and pounded their life away while serving time in the Big House. Stone walls rising 150 feet above the floor of the quarry jutted out in layers created by the daily dynamiting for the limestone.

Rumor had it that a spring was struck by one of the prisoners, with a sledge hammer, but I heard years later that it was a misplaced dynamite charge, at any rate it filled the quarry so quickly that they couldn't get any of the trucks or equipment out. The water that filled the quarry was emerald green with swirling eddies, scattered across the surface. On the bottom, the mining cars and rails were still there, along with numerous trucks, a model T Ford, a legendary safe full of money from a robbery, and two cranes. Many of the kids that drowned in the quarry were never found because their bodies were hooked on something, 150 feet down.

I was 9 years old that hot summer when the brilliant green water was a lure for all the kids on the West Side. All but the Harris boys, and they were absolutely forbidden to go to the quarry.

"Have you boys been to Prisoner's Quarry?" Mother caught Jerry, Leroy and David coming down the embankment from the railroad tracks on Central Avenue one hot afternoon. They were sunburned and Leroy's hair was damp.

"No Awk, we were out looking for bottles." Jerry gave the boys the eye.

"Yeah Awk, we was lookin' for bottles." David grinned.

"Bottles my ass, you slicky, but you no slicky I! You were at the quarry." She whacked Jerry on the top of his head and pointed her finger toward the house.

"All of you can go home and stay there until Clyde gets off work. There'll be hell to pay then, I can tell you that!"

It was a few days later when we heard the wail of the emergency squad coming out Central Avenue, it happened at least three times during the summer. Mother and I and Maw ran out to the street and shaded our eyes as the squad turned West on McKinley into the sunset.

"They were towin' a boat. Some mother'll be crying tonight." Maw predicted.

"Buddy said he saw Jerry and the boys walking on the tracks last Sunday," Maw said.

Mother looked closely at me, "Did you know anything about that?"

"David is only 7 years old; Jerry wouldn't let him go to the quarry, would he?" I didn't tell her that I knew about Jerry and Leroy going, though. I was afraid to tell her how they had made Earl jump from one of the ledges and he nearly drowned. Earl didn't like the water, and the sun blistered his fair skin. One summer he wore shorts and his legs were iridescent white, like the underbelly of a frog. I knew he wouldn't ever go back, he was too afraid.

The quarry set the status quo for the boys on the West Side. The high divers were revered by the other kids, and young as he was, David was one of them.

He could jack knife from the top ledges and stay under water until he came bursting to the surface like a rocket, gasping for air. Leroy on the other hand was a jumper, he never liked going in head first, especially when there was a lot of kids diving around him.

Jerry wasn't afraid to dive but his nose bled every time he went down ten feet, which probably saved his life since he had a penchant for getting into trouble. Maw loved David best of all; she swore he was the reincarnation of her dead brother Watson.

"Watson worked for the railroad and he was so good looking all the women was chasing after him." Maw said.

"He always wore a red bandanna around his neck when he was working."

"What happened to him?" I asked her wearily every time she told me about Watson.

"He caught hold of the side of a locomotive as it was slowing down for the roundhouse and he lost his footing and fell under the wheels." Maw wiped behind her glasses with the tip of her apron as she always did when she cried.

"David is the spittin' image of Watson, and he's got that same sweet disposition he had." I tell you," Maw banged her cane on the floor for emphasis. "That boy *is* Watson."

It was 91 degrees that late afternoon in July as I helped set the table for dinner, and Maw and Mother stood cooking over the hot stove in the kitchen.

"Jo, go over to Littler's and fetch David, I need a loaf of bread and I promised him a dime next time he went to the store for me." Maw waved me off, "Are you goin' or not?" I need it today, not next week."

David wasn't at Littler's. Mrs. Littler told me he had been to her house earlier that day and wanted Tommy to go swimming with him. When I saw the boys rounding the corner at West Side Motors on River Street I was relieved, but David wasn't with them.

"Where's David?" I asked.

"Not with us, we've been to the Asylum visiting the walnuts." Jerry did his gagging act but stopped when he saw I wasn't laughing.

"I can't find David." I told him what Mrs. Littler said.

"Oh hell Jo, maybe he went fishing with Tuna, they go over to Grandview sometimes."

"I saw Tuna walking past the house just before I left." I said.

"Jo! He wouldn't go to the quarry without us!" Leroy said in his loudest voice, the worried voice he used when he was upset. His eyebrows rose, "Would he?"

"Did you look over in the ball park?" Earl asked. We ran to the park and it was empty, the heat had driven everyone home to the shade or the swimming holes, or the quarry. We walked home in silence, each of us had his own guilt to carry, we were all responsible for David, he was the baby, next to Marilyn Rose.

We heard it in the distance, a mournful wailing. It grew and grew until it sped past us and turned on McKinley Avenue heading west. It was the emergency squad, and it was towing a boat. There was another drowning at the quarry.

I ran to the Central Avenue overpass and scrambled up the embankment, not feeling the cinders strike my legs as they rained from the top, and ran down the tracks toward the quarry.

I was stepping on every other railroad tie as I ran, hoping I wouldn't miss one and fall on my face. It wouldn't be the first time. The quarry was a good two miles down the tracks but I made it in record time. When I got there, a crowd was gathered around the squad.

"The last time I saw him he was jumping off that ledge up there." A thin boy in cut off jeans with his hair still dripping stood talking to the rescue squad. He was trembling even though it was 91 degrees.

"He hit the water, and I saw him go down, way down into the dark green. I never saw him dive that far before, he always stayed pretty close to the surface."

"Who was on the ledge?" I was so afraid to ask.

"Was it David Harris?" I touched his arm and he was crying when he turned around.

"You relation to those Harris boys?" he asked me, and I shook my head.

"It wasn't David, it was my little brother, Billy." he sobbed.

Billy was just about David's age with the same blonde curly hair and blue eyes. They were in the same class together at Chicago Avenue Elementary.

Relief swept through me like a torch and left me feeling dizzy and weak. I had to sit down on the dirty ground until I stopped shaking.

Then I felt guilt, for being glad it wasn't David. Everyone was sitting at the kitchen table when I walked in, except David. I went to the sink and washed my hands, worried all over again, wondering where he could be.

"Has anyone seen David yet? I asked as I sat down to eat.

"Seen him? He went to Dolders for me, to get that bread, no thanks to you." Maw pointed her fork at me, "They is them that does, and them that doesn't, and you are a "doesn't," girl. I saw you runnin' down the railroad tracks like a damn fairy when you was supposed to be finding David for me."

A police car went flying down McKinley with his siren blaring, headed west into the sunset.

"I wonder where he's going in such a hurry, probably out to that damn quarry." Mother smiled as David walked in the back door with a bag of groceries from Dolders.

"Come and eat, baby, I have your plate all ready," she said to him.

I went around the table and hugged him hard, and kissed his cheek.

"What's that for?" he wiped his cheek on his shoulder.

"For you, just because," I dipped my head to avoid the stares I was getting from everyone around the table. I knew they wouldn't understand why I felt like crying and how grateful I was that David was sitting across from me now, with a biscuit in one hand and a milky mustache on his upper lip. My heart ached for the boy who was on the bottom of Prisoners Quarry, but I thanked God for his special protection of those damn Harris boys.

Wheels

My father was always protective of me, and our house was full of daring young men on Saturday night whose stories about their quick-wit behind the wheel of a stock car, racing 95 miles an hour, made my heart pound. He would let me hang over the front seat of his 41' Plymouth while he spun the wheel, taking curves easily at 75. I studied his foot movements on the pedals, when he braked, and when he gave it the gas.

"You always want to give it gas on the curves baby," he told me, "hug the inside corner then punch her down for the stretch." He pointed to an automobile in the distance, his cigarette clasped between thumb and forefinger. "Always make sure you have enough speed to pass the guy you're coming up on. Nine times out of ten when you're neck to neck with him, he'll decide to race you. He might want you to play chicken, see how long you stay in your lane before hitting the curve. Course, you could back down and let him win." His wink told me he would never let that happen, and every time he passed a car after that, I wondered if we would get to play chicken.

What I didn't learn from him, I picked up from his racing buddies. "Lotsa times a guy wants to race you at a stop light, he needs to prove he's got the engine, you know? Don't even look at him. Then when the light turns green, let em' eat your smoke." Dominic always had good solid advice for me. He was one of my driving instructors when I turned 16.

By then my father had settled into a nice 52 Chevrolet and he let me have his 41' Plymouth with the flathead 6 cylinder engine. I was the only girl in our high school to drive, and the boys were constantly challenging me to race against them. Of course I did, and I always won.

They started hanging out at the house to talk to my father about carburetors and crankshafts, and before long I was more popular than the homecoming queen.

One day I was driving through town with dad, when a black and chrome Harley pulled up beside us at a traffic light.

"Tell me something, will you?" His eyes had a faraway look, like he was visiting a memory.

"What?" I nudged him, "Why do you look so serious?"

"Remember that guy, Steve somebody that had the motorcycle?" How could I forget him?

"Yeah? What about him?" I knew what the question was and I hid my grin.

"Where did he take you that night?" He glanced at me with his eyebrows pulled together.

"You know," I laughed, "you ask me that question once a year? Someday, I'll tell you."

Two years later I sat on his bed in the hospital and we both knew without words that he was leaving me at every tick of the clock. But I had something to tell him before he was gone.

"Hey," my voice trembled and I turned my head away so he wouldn't see my tears.

"Remember that guy? Steve somebody, that had the motorcycle?"

"Yeah...where...did he take you that night, baby?"

"We went...."I willed my voice to speak over the lump in my throat, "downtown, past the RKO Grand. It was all lit up dad,...like a big jewel, the entire block, all those beautiful lights, it was like Christmas, and everything was reflected on the river, even the big moon."

"You should have...told me that night, I was ready to give him a Joe Louis."

"Did you think I was going to give him my famous figure eight kiss?"

"The thought did cross my mind." He closed his eyes, and I fell to earth. "Baby...don't cry, nothing...is forever. And don't you forget how much I always...loved you."

God...how could I.

The Ghosty Old House

Mother likes to tell people that I walked when I was eight months old. I didn't believe it when she told me; I had to verify it with Aunt Ethyl.

"It's true honey pie. You were eight months old, no bigger than a maggot, and there you were walking. Most babies are just sittin' up good by then." she told me.

She had my crib in the back bedroom with a door leading to her room. When the whistle blew at the Asylum on the hilltop at 6:00 a.m. dad got up for work, and so did I. I don't know how old I was the first time I climbed over that crib railing and dropped to the floor, but I do remember why I needed to do it.

I was being poked and tickled, uncovered and examined, whispered to, and on one occasion, lifted out of the crib by unseen hands. I could feel myself floating, while all around my bed gray misty faces peered down at me. They stayed there until dawn seeped around the edges of the green blinds and filled the room with soft morning light. A friend of mine told me recently that *they*, were probably Aliens, but we always thought they were ghosts of past relatives.

Whatever they were they have always been there, along with all the other phantoms and spirits of dogs and cats and dark forms that walk in the upstairs hall, both day and night. When the boys were very young, Buddy had a game he liked to play with them.

"I'll give a quarter to anyone, who will stay in the front bedroom for five minutes, in the dark." He'd hold out the quarter in his palm, the overhead light in the hall gleaming off it.

"You can knock when you want out, if you can't stay that long." Earl was desperate for the quarter, but he was terrified of the dark and what it might hold, just waiting to grab him.

"Will you do it Earl?" Buddy always urged him

"I dunno. I might do it." Earl hedged. "And you'll let me out just as soon as I knock on the damn door?"

"Swear to God," Buddy held his hand up and crossed his chest.

"I dunno." Earl shook his head and gnawed on his thumb nail.

"Oh come on Zeta, are you a girl or a boy?" Jerry liked to call Earl "Zeta," and "Nell," it made him mad as hell.

"Perch on this!" Earl's middle finger shot up in Jerry's face.

"Well? You gonna do it or not!" Buddy urged. "We don't have all night."

"All right! I'll do it. I'm not scared of those goddamn ghosts."

"That's the spirit, Zeta!" Jerry shrieked.

Buddy slowly opened the bedroom door. Of course it creaked. Inside it was pitch dark. This was the bedroom where Pernoon had seen the giant German shepherd with the red glowing eyes sitting by her bed when she was a young woman. This was the room with the big hole in the ceiling that showed the rafters in the dark attic. The one with the people whisperin, when you tried to sleep. This was *my* room.

"Go on in, Earl." Leroy urged him.

Earl took a deep breath, like the pearl divers in the islands, and stepped into the darkness. Jerry put his lips against the door and whispered.

"Raaaw neck and bloody booones." Earl started knocking frantically on the door as Buddy was closing it. He never did get the quarter.

David was the youngest of the boys and from the time he was born, he had fearlessness in him, it was as if he knew he was protected by a greater force. He was never afraid of the dark, it was his friend. Buddy never offered him the quarter, he knew better.

When David was three years old mother entered him in a beauty contest, Eva and I took him on the bus to Central High School in the auditorium. Everywhere he went people stopped us on the street to look at him. His hair was a golden mass of curls and when he laughed his deep blue eyes sparkled and formed dimples at the corners.

Mother had dressed him in a mint stripped cotton playsuit for the contest and the judges were walking around looking at the babies, they filled the huge stage at the auditorium. I was shocked to see the other babies dressed in elaborate costumes, one was a king with a velvet cape and gold crown, and another was dressed as a caveman.

The judges said David was the prettiest baby they had ever seen, he looked angelic. They gave him third place. They told us he would have placed first easily if he had been in costume.

When he was eight years old he brought a friend home to spend the night. The next morning at breakfast mother asked David where his friend was.

"He jumped out the window at 2:00 this morning; he said he couldn't stay in our house." David wrinkled his brows together, "Shoot, Awk, why won't any of my friends stay over night?"

"Maybe Grandpa didn't like him," Leroy cackled, until mother shot him a lethal stare.

Twelve years later, David, who was pure born and unable to see the evil in men or fear the darkness, signed up for Viet Nam where he saw friends butchered and he himself was wounded and sent home.

He immediately returned to Viet Nam, with a death wish, after coming home and finding his wife was pregnant with another man's child. He nearly got his wish when he lost control of an Army truck on a mountain road, and it ran over him. He came home wired like a puppet, and after three months in the hospital, he stayed at the old house with mother and dad.

David was shattered in spirit, and everyone was careful to speak softly and tiptoe down the hall when he was napping. He had been home for a week before he was able to hold a cup of coffee in his hands without spilling it, and some of the color was beginning to come back into his cheeks.

One evening he was sitting upstairs with dad in the big bedroom telling him one of the endless stories of battles fought and comrades lost, as if by telling it he could shed the ugliness from his memory.

It was midnight before he uncurled himself from the old wing back chair and went into the bathroom to shave and shower for bed. A few minutes later we heard him scream. He came running down the hall and literally threw himself into my father's arms.

"What the hell?" Dad said, as he held him in his arms.

Everyone in the house ran to see what was going on. When David could speak again, he told us how he had looked into the mirror and seen the shower curtain standing straight out in the air behind him.

Maw quickly crossed herself, "There'll be a death in the family, mark my words."

Pernoon agreed; she was born with a veil over her face, a thin layer of skin, and she had the "gift."

"Pernoon can see things that nobody else can see." Mother told me one time.

No one in our family disputed what David had seen, except his doctor. "It's his nerves, he thinks he really does see these things." he shrugged. When David told Maw, she was livid.

"Nerves, my ass! Tell that idiot doctor to come and spend the night *here*!"

Maw's husband Ike still comes home every morning at 3:25 a.m., stomping up the steps in his big engineer boots from a weekly run on the New York Central railroad on old number 42. He turns at the landing and heads down the hall to the back bedroom where he slams the door, knocking the hall clock askew. Aside from the fact that he's making enough noise to wake the dead, let me mention here and now; he is.. Dead, I mean.

When I was five years old and Cousin Joan was eight, mother called Zeta to come and take her to see Dr. Eckard over on Broad Street. Jerry was a new baby and she was convinced that he had "short growth," an old wives' tale that will kill a baby if it is not treated. Joan was recovering from the croup and she wasn't supposed to be outside even though it was a hot summer day.

"Mommy went downtown this morning," mother told Zeta. "She thought Jo and Joan were going with us to the doctor's office. I don't think we'll be gone that long and little Annie is right next door. I think we can leave them here for an hour, don't you?" Zeta looked dubious, but she pulled Joan aside and shook her finger in her face.

"Don't you dare go outside for anything, you understand?" Zeta cautioned her as they left. Joan had brought her toy phones and she told me to go upstairs and sit on the top step and she sat at the bottom. She dialed and called me and I pretended to answer, then I called her.

The upstairs was dark because all the green blinds were drawn to keep out the heat. I was sitting by the banister that ran along the upstairs hall that led to Maw's room, and her door was closed.

That end of the hall was thrown into total darkness, but something back there kept grabbing my attention. It was the door, the knob was rattling softly. I started down the steps but Joan stopped me.

"No! Go back up there so I can call you," she said."

"I don't want to. I don't like it up there, it's dark and something is in Maw's room."

"Jo, you're such a big baby! You get back up there right now!" I couldn't do it. She took hold of my arm and pulled me up the steps.

"Stay right here and don't come down again."She dialed me on her phone but I couldn't answer, I was watching the door to Maw's room as it slowly opened. I could see that there was light coming in around the blind at her window, and then the light was blocked by a dark mass that filled the doorway. It was like black smoke that poured forward and then folded back against itself, like a huge inchworm. It reached out and touched the far end of the banister in the hall and the light from Maw's window framed it as it moved away from her doorway, advancing steadily in my direction. I screamed but I couldn't move.

"What is the matter with you?" Joan came stomping up the steps, but when she saw what was in the hall she screamed too, and ran back down, leaving me alone while *it* swelled and receded, swelled and receded, bringing itself closer to me each time.

I thought Joan ran out the front door but she bravely pounded back up the steps, took a firm hold on my dress sleeve and dragged me downstairs. As soon as we could make our legs work properly we both scrambled to the front door. It wouldn't open. The knob was loose, you had to push it in and turn it to open the door. The knob spun and spun while we screamed and screamed, listening to the steps creaking under the weight of *it,* as *it* came after us. At last the knob caught and we flung the door open and ran outside. Ruby Imes, a girl down the street, was walking past the house and she stopped when she saw us.

"You guys look scared to death, what happened to you?"

"We saw something in the hall and it chased us, it was black and awful."

Joan babbled while my heart pounded against my dress. Ruby wanted to go in and see what was scaring us but at that moment mother and Zeta pulled in front of the house. Zeta was ready to spank Joan until she saw our faces; we were both chalk white and crying. When I told mother what I had seen, she shook her head.

"You didn't see anything honey, the wind probably blew the door open, that's all."

I might have bought into that theory except for one thing. There wasn't a whisper of wind that summer day, even the green blinds in her room were not moving at all, as they did if there was even a breath of air, and also, Maw's doorknob was just like the one in the front door, you had to pull back on it and rattle the knob until it caught. It was a long time before I could I go upstairs alone or be in Maw's room without waiting for the closet door to open and *it* to come inching out.

It's not unusual to awaken in the darkest hour and hear a loud party going on downstairs. Laughing and talking; chairs scraping on the bare floor, silverware and glasses clinking. If you rush down the steps as mother has on several occasions, her housecoat standing out behind her, you will find the house dark and still, with only the tick of the Grandfather clock in the hall.

In the past, family members that died had their caskets in the front room parlor for a three day showing. There is a cold spot in that area of the room now. I know, I sat in it one hot July thinking it was air conditioning and remembering with a jolt that mother didn't have air conditioning. When I told her about it she shrugged her shoulders.

"Don't worry Jo," she waved me off. "It's only my daddy, and he won't hurt you."

When I was thirteen, even dad, who refused to believe in ghosts, and was the first to try and find the true meaning of it all, had an incident that he couldn't explain.

He was sick one night and decided to sleep downstairs on the sofa in the front room. He told me about it reluctantly, with mother urging him on.

"I was having a hard time sleeping, and I turned over and I looked this woman right in the face, she was leaning over from behind the sofa, staring at me. She looked like Maw's mother in law, Delila. She was tall as a man, with black hair twisted in the back, black eyes and a sharp nose. It kind of gave me a start, you know, because the sofa was against the wall!"

"What did you do?" I could feel goose bumps raising the fine hairs on my arms. If *he* admitted to seeing a ghost, they'd be sure to get me.

"I went in the kitchen and got a drink of water and started upstairs." He said.

"I felt something pulling on the leg of my pants and I looked down. She was on the stairs, grabbing at my leg, you know I wouldn't tell you that, if it wasn't true."

By now my hair was standing straight up on my head and so was mother's.

He hesitated and mother elbowed him, "Go on, finish telling her what you told me."

"I kicked my foot at her, but she kept on coming. I went on into the bathroom and when I was done washing I got into bed and your mother was asleep. I was trying to do the same, but this thing kept pulling the covers off the bed. Finally she stopped I was drifting off to sleep when I heard this tapping sound on the floor by the bed." He stopped and took a deep breath, looking away from me.

"What? Tell us what it was." I needed to know.

"Baby, I don't want to tell you." He went over and poured himself a cup of coffee and sat down. "Some things are better left unsaid."

"Tell her what you told me, Clyde." Mother elbowed me. "He told me this already, and I believe him because it happened to Leroy. You know your father wouldn't lie, don't you?"

I shook my head, I had never known him to lie to me. After a while he went on.

"I got up to see what it was, and my damn shoes," he threw his hands over his head and looked bewildered, "they were walking around the room. I grabbed em' and put em' back under the bed, and after a while everything was quiet for the rest of the night."

"What was making your shoes walk?" my upper lip hung forward like a duck's bill.

"I don't know baby, I've never seen anything like that in my life." He lit a Lucky Strike and his hand trembled. I knew he wasn't afraid of anything he could get by the collar, or explain its existence, but I think this went beyond the realm of his comprehension and it freaked him out.

"And this morning, when I looked under the bed where I put those shoes last night? They wasn't there. They was over by your mother's side of the bed, and I sure didn't do that"

If anyone else had told me that story I would have called them a bare-faced liar. In all the years he lived there in that old house it was the only time he ever told me anything like that, and I believed him.

Going Back

When I was fifteen, Eva was in an automobile accident. She was in a car with a girl from school, a wild girl named Alice, that I didn't like, and the girl's boyfriend Justin, was drinking. They were going to see a movie, The Rose Tattoo, and Eva begged me to come with them as we stood in front of Starling Jr. High School. I reminded her that mother wouldn't let me ride in anyone's car, especially with a teenage driver.

"Just tell your mother you're going to stay all night with Eva." Alice said. "I can't lie to her, she'd find out." I wouldn't be seen with Alice anyway, I thought she was trash. I couldn't understand Eva's friendship with her; Alice looked like a hedgehog with her hair growing low on her forehead nearly to her eyebrows and her little curved hands like claws.

"I lie to my mother all the time, and she never catches me." Alice shrugged.

I turned to Eva. "Why don't you stay with me tonight, and you and I can take the bus downtown and see that movie?" Eva opened her mouth to speak but Alice interrupted her.

"She wants to see the movie with Danny, Justin's friend. I got them together last week at my house, didn't I?" She winked at Eva and snickered.

"I was going to tell you all about him, really I was. He is so cute, and I'd like to see him tonight." Eva whispered, "Don't be mad."

I was hurt and I walked away from her, tears stinging my eyes. She had always told me her secrets just as I had always told her all of mine. Now all that had changed.

"I'll see you tomorrow," she called after me. "Maybe I'll stay over and we can go downtown."

I heard Justin peel rubber as he turned on Central Avenue from Broad Street. It was the last time I ever talked to her. That night he missed a curve on Clime Road.

I was up all that night, I couldn't sleep, and when I finally did, mother was standing in my bedroom.

"Jo?" She sounded serious, "Come downstairs, I have something to tell you."

Eva was in the hospital with a broken arm and internal injuries she told me. The police couldn't find her parents until later; they were in a bar on Broad Street. Alice was killed instantly, and Justin wasn't expected to live. But I knew Eva would be fine, she had to be.

I wasn't allowed to go and see her at Mt. Carmel Hospital, mother said it was best, but after two days I took my bike one night and went anyway. I sneaked past the desk and took the elevator up to the second floor and found her room. She was sleeping with a white tunic wrapped around her head and her left arm was in a cast. I sat down in the chair by the bed and spoke to her.

"Hey, it's me," I whispered "I'm sorry I was away for three weeks this summer in Michigan with Joan and her parents, you had no-one to be with. But I'm here now and I'll never leave you again, I promise. You'll be fine. You have to be, because I love you so much."

That's when I saw that they had pinned a Madonna Metal on her bandaged right arm. With an electric shock I realized she had been given the last rites. How could they? I was angry, Eva would have been too. We had watched the nuns coming out of the Holy Family chapel on Broad Street and walking in two's across the street, their black robes blowing like huge Raven's wings in the wind.

I knew how much she hated the pomp and circumstance of the church. Well just leave it to the damn *Catlicks* to declare you dead when you were going to be up and around in a few days, I thought. All at once she sat up and opened her eyes. I breathed a sigh of relief; I knew she was going to be all right now. I would take care of her until she was on her feet again.

"Mother," she screamed, and I tried to get her to see that I was there, but the nurse came in and made me leave the room.

"I'll see you tomorrow," I said. "I love you, hurry and get well."

As I left the room a loud buzzer rang. Nurses were running down the hall with a blue machine on wheels as I got on the elevator. It was dark when I rode into the front yard and Buddy ran out to meet me.

"Did you hear?" He said, "Did you hear? Eva just died." He said....And so did I.

Mother and dad never went out drinking again.

In a trance I went downtown to Lazarus department store where we used to go when we were kids, trying on all the hats in the French Room, and bought the clothes for her burial. A light blue wool skirt, a pink cardigan and pretty silk slippers, and I added some things she had loved to borrow from me.

After the funeral I walked around in a tranquilized daze, it was the only way I could live. I couldn't eat and I couldn't sleep. Mother would come in my room and rock me in her arms like a baby, and she slept with me held tight against her, until I could feel the pounding of her heart with my own. Eva had been in all my classes at school. We sang in the glee club together, she was soprano and I was alto. Suddenly the seat next to mine was empty. The pink sweater we always laughingly fought over still had her Evening In

Paris perfume on the sleeve. I slept in it every night for a year.

One hot summer night eight months after Eva was gone, my little sister Marilyn was sleeping on a small bed in my bedroom when she woke up screaming. Mother ran in and turned on the lights.

"I saw Eva." Marilyn was crying, "she was standing by Jo's bed and she bent over and kissed her, then she went out of the window like a puff of smoke when I screamed."

Marilyn was five years old and we thought she was dreaming. The next morning my bedroom was filled with the fragrance of Evening In Paris. Thirty years later I wrote her a poem.

> *We were fifteen when you died,*
> *so close we cast a single shadow, how I cried.*
> *I still have the sweater you loaned me,*
> *30 years ago, would you believe?*
> *Your Evening In Paris fragrance,*
> *still lingers on the sleeve?*
> *I remember your auburn hair,*
> *falling careless across your shoulder,*
> *You haunt my dreams,*
> *where you are young forever,*
> *And I am growing older.*
> *Time owes me much and I will have my due,*
> *It owes me youth, the years we lost, it owes me you.*

The old house sits quiet now, except for the spirits of Maw and my father, joining those whose energy still lives within its walls. I moved to Florida but Leroy remained a bachelor and he has chosen to stay home with mother and care for her. Last year when I went back home for a visit, Leroy told me how he had been taking a shower when he saw a dark shadow against the clear shower curtain; he thought it was his cat, Serena.

"I thought she was casting a big shadow and then I felt this sudden stinging on my left side, and when I got out of the shower I had four long red marks on my side, like claws."

Leroy has grown into a quiet unassuming man, and he was clearly embarrassed when he showed me the four long scratch marks across his side. I chalked it up as an acccident, until I fell down the steps twice while I was there. The second fall nearly broke my arm.

Mother takes it all in stride, as she has always done with everything in her life. "Oh hell, *they* ought to know you, Jo. After all, you lived here most of your life. Give them a few days and see what happens," she said matter of factly.

I have not slept in that house alone since I was five, and always with the quilt pulled over my head. But when mother had to go in the hospital for some tests she called me.

"Jo, I have to go into the hospital, and see what the hell is hurting my stomach. Its ulcers, but the doctors have to pay for their Mercedes, so they're running some tests." She never goes to the doctor, she still looks young at 82, and to prove it, she will throw herself on the floor and in a contorted position, she begins singing,

"Ohhhh, an old man he is old, and an old man he is gray, get away old man, get awayyyy."

"I want to make sure Leroy eats," she told me, "he works so hard in that steel factory. He's all skin and bones. I said if the cannibals ever got a hold of him they wouldn't bother to cook him, they'd let him go. I want you to cook for him while I'm in the hospital, will you do that?"

"Don't worry about it mother," I said, "I'll be there and take care of everything." When she had told me she was going into the hospital for tests I knew it could be serious so I took the next flight out of Tampa.

I knew Leroy would be leaving the house before the sun came up and I would be alone there with the ghost of grandpa and the thing that had clawed Leroy, and the dog with the red eyes and whatever in the hell had caused that kid to jump out of David's window, and the shower curtain rising and falling, and the black smoke in the hallway upstairs, and it was more than I could stand to think about.

I tore at the paper napkin in my lap and bit my lower lip as my plane landed that night in Columbus.

It was twilight when my taxi pulled in front of the dark house, I couldn't see any lights on inside. I set the suitcase by the front door and rang the bell in case Leroy was upstairs in the bathroom. Stuck in the door was a note from him.

"Jo, I had to work overtime. The key is in the usual place. See you soon."

I found the key under the Hens and Chickens pot on the porch. My hand was trembling; I was five years old again and scared. I was always scared. Minutes ticked by while I stood with my head pressed against the glass panel on the door, the same door that Joan and I couldn't get open that afternoon so long ago. I could almost see the two little girls screaming on the other side of the glass, spinning that silver door knob, trying to escape.

I looked out at the front gate where I had stood when I was eight years old crying over Millie and scared to confront her. But I had confronted her, and it had dissolved my fear.

I remembered something else too. If there really were ghosts, then dad was there in the old house as well, his spirit, and Maw's, and Eva's and Pernoon's. I had loved them all so much, and they had loved me. I took a deep breath, inserted the key and walked into the dark house.

"Hello?" I called to them, "It's me, and I'm home."

The End

The McKinley Avenue Primer

Webster's Dictionary: PRIMER: A textbook that gives the first principals of any subject.
As an Analogy:
In logic, the inference that certain admitted resemblances imply Probable further similarities

A woman can throw out more on a spoon than a man can bring in with a shovel.

He must of had poor raisins....Bad manners.

Her mouth looked like a split in a pumpkin....Too much red lipstick

The Moon's on its back....A bad moon, evil abounds.

They is them that does and them that doesn't....Some can do it, some can't.

Puttin' on the dog....Acting like you have more than you really do.

Ready for market....A very fat person.

No use cryin' over spilt milk....Can't do anything about it now.

Bible totter....Preacher.

Like pissin' in the ocean....It won't make any difference.

Pissin' in the wind....It's gonna come back on you.

Puckerin' up....crying.

Raining pitch forks and broom handles....Big storm.

Naked as a jay bird.....No clothes on.

As God is my witness....telling the absolute truth.

Knocked up higher than a kite....9 months pregnant.

A pumpkin on the vine...2-3 months pregnant.

Meaner than Grant burnin' Richmond....very, very mean, extra mean Sonsabitches....All of them.

No use in stirrin' up the pot...Gossiping.

Here comes the devil slidin' on his ass....Someone running to tell you bad news.

That don't mean Jackshit...It means absolutely nothing.

I mightas well....It's gonna happen anyway.

Happier than a hog on ice....extremely happy.

Not a pot to piss in nor a window to throw it out of....Extra poor.

He ain't got the powder to blow out his own brains....He hasn't got anything.

He'd steal Christ from the cross and go back for the nails....A chronic thief.

Better know which side your bread's buttered on....Better stay out of trouble.

Poorer than a church mouse....Very poor.

Sposin'....What if.

Yankee brains....Stupid.

Dog piss....Weak coffee.

That'll put hair on your chest....Strong coffee.

Crib robber....Older man with a younger girl.

Lyin' through his teeth....Lying out of spite.

Runnin' with his tail between his legs....Coward.

Yellah.... Extra bad Coward.

Shouldn't oughta'....Shouldn't have.

Cowboys and Indians.....My father and Cal fighting others in a bar.

You're damned if you do and damned if you don't....Can't go either way.

Throwin' good money after bad....gambling or buying something worthless.

Using a little hand oil....A good spanking.

Lockin' lips....Kissing.

Pert'n near....Almost

When the Ghost walks...Getting unexpected money.

When the Eagle shits....Getting the pension check from the government.

Yankee Bastards....Yankee Bastards.

Kara Seen....Kerosene.

He's Green....Doesn't know any better yet.

Ain't spittin' nickels....Doesn't have unlimited money..

Hittin' the box....Dying.

He's not worth the labor it took him to be born....Worthless, lazy.

Makin' do....Leftovers.

Puddle Jumper....Junk car.

A day late and a dollar short....Not enough.

A pig in a poke....Buying something you can't see.

A visit from Grandma.....Monthly period.

Wet behind the ears....Too young to know anything.

A little long in the tooth....Older than she say's she is.

Clever as a pocket in a shirt....Mother telling cousin Emmit that 7 year old Earl was clever enough to put his gold Hamiliton watch back together again ...and he did!.

Made in United States
North Haven, CT
04 November 2022